Young Reader's FIRST PICTURE DICTIONARY

Illustrated by Al Buntin & Rikki O'Neill of Wizard Art.
Courtesy of Bernard Thornton Artists.

© Published by Peter Haddock Limited, Bridlington, UK.

Aa

A is the first letter of the alphabet.
A dog is an animal.
Digger is **a** dog.

ABLE

You are **able** to read this book.
Babies are not **able** to read.
Able means that you can do something.

ABOUT

Digger Dog is **about** to have his supper.
Digger is going to have his supper very soon.

ABOVE

Billy Budgie flies **above** the baby's head.
Look **above** the baby's head to see him.

ABROAD

Aunty Ivy lives **abroad**.
She lives in a foreign country.

ABSENT

David was **absent** from school today.
He did not go to school.
He is away today.

ACCEPT

Sammy Seal has invited everyone to a party. Will they all **accept**?
Will they all be at the party?

ACCIDENT

Uncle Harry has had an **accident**.
He has fallen down the stairs.

ACORN

Watch Squeaky Squirrel eating an **acorn**. An **acorn** is the seed of an oak tree.

ACROBAT

Batty Bat thinks he is an **acrobat**.
He can hang upside down.

ACROSS

Clarence Cat walked **across** the street.
He walked to the other side of the street.
His house is **across** the street.

ACT

When we are in the school play we **act**.
Would you like to **act** a part in the play?

ACTIVE

Elly Elephant is very **active**.
She is busy cleaning her trunk.

ADD

Can you **add**?
2 + 2 = 4
4 + 4 = 8
When you **add** 4 and 2,
you have 6.

ADDRESS

This is Bertie Bear's **address**.
This is where he lives.

ADEQUATE

Bertie Bear must eat an **adequate**
amount of food before
he hibernates.
He must eat enough before he goes
to sleep for the winter.

ADJECTIVE

An **adjective** describes a noun
(the name of anything).
Olly Owl has shining feathers
(the **adjective** is 'shining').

ADMIRE

Billy Budgie
likes to
admire
himself in the
mirror.
He likes
looking at himself.

ADMISSION

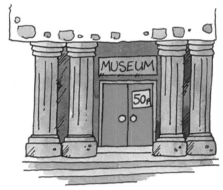

Admission to the museum is 50p.
It costs 50p to go inside.

ADMIT

Two tickets will **admit** Daffy Duck
and Lucy Lamb to the circus. They
can sit at the ringside.

ADULT

Your mother is an **adult**.
Your father is
one too.
They are
grown-up
people.

ADVANCE

Look at all these ants as they
advance.
They all move forward.

ADVENTURE

An **adventure** is an exciting or
unusual event.
Peter had a ride in a helicopter.
That was an **adventure**.

ADVERTISE

People **advertise** things to sell.
They put notices in newspapers and
shop windows.
This is called an **advertisement**.

AFRAID

Olly Owl is not **afraid** of the dark.
He can see in the night.
He is not scared.

AFTER

B comes **after** A.
D comes **after** C.
Clarence Cat chases **after**
Missy Mouse.

AGAIN

Sing the song **again**.
Sing it one more time.

AGAINST

My bike leans **against** the wall.
My bike touches the wall.
We played
against
each other
in the
football
match.
We were
on opposite
sides.

AGE

What is
your **age**?
How old are you?
Twins are the same **age**.

AGO

Years **ago** there were no motor cars
or trucks.
In past years people had horses and
carriages.

AGREE

Daniel Dwarf and Eric Elf **agree**.
They do not argue. They think alike.

AIR

We breathe **air**.
Air is all around us.
We cannot see **air** but, when the
wind blows, we feel the **air** moving.
Eddy Eagle flies in the **air**.

AIRCRAFT

An **aircraft** is a machine that flies
through the air.
Arnold **Aircraft** flies high in the
sky.

AIRLINE

Arnold Aircraft carries passengers
for a famous **airline**.

AIRPORT

An **airport** is a place where aircraft
take off and land.

AJAR

Albert Ape left the door **ajar**.
The door is slightly open.

ALARM

A loud or sudden noise **alarms** us.
We think something may be wrong.
Andy Ambulance sounds an **alarm**
as he speeds on his way.

ALARM CLOCK

The bell on an **alarm clock** rings
to signal to us that it is time to
get up.

ALBATROSS
An **albatross** is a
very large, web-footed
seabird.
An **albatross** can fly long
distances.

ALBUM

An **album** is a book with blank
pages for holding photographs,
pictures or stamps etc.
Annie Antelope has an **album** of
autographs.

ALCOHOL

Alcohol is the colourless liquid in
wine, beer and spirits which makes
them intoxicating.

ALIKE

Identical twins are very much **alike**.
Jane and her mother walk **alike**.

ALIVE

The car hit the dog but the dog is still
alive.
The dog is not dead.

ALL

All spiders have eight legs.
All horses have hooves.
Almost **all** little children
like sweets.

ALLEY

An **alley** is a very narrow street that
has buildings on both sides.

ALLIGATOR

Ally **Alligator**
has four short legs
and a long tail.
She crawls along the ground and
she swims in the warm river.

ALLOCATE

The teacher will **allocate** a desk to
each child.
The teacher will tell each child where
to sit.

ALLOW

Mother will **allow** me to watch
television.
She will not **allow** me to eat too
many sweets.

ALMOST

It is **almost** time to go to bed.
It is nearly bedtime.
Ninety-nine is **almost** one hundred.

ALONE

One boy stood **alone** on the hill.
One girl **alone** can do this puzzle.
She can do it on her own.

ALPHABET

This is a group of letters used in writing a language.
The English **alphabet** is -
A B C D E F G H I J K L M N O
P Q R S T U V W X Y Z.

ALPINE

Alpine plants grow on high mountains like the Swiss **Alps**. **Alpine** skiers ski down high mountains.

ALREADY

You are ten minutes late **already**.
The children have **already** gone to the party.

ALSO

Daniel Dwarf has a pair of boots.
I have a pair of boots **also**.
I have a pair of boots too.

ALTER

Belinda Ballerina's dress does not fit.
She will **alter** it.
She will make it fit.

ALTHOUGH

Although the boy had been told to tidy his room he had not done so.
In spite of being told to do so the boy had not tidied his room.

ALTOGETHER

Altogether, we found ten different shells.
Counting all, we found ten different shells.
The building was **altogether** destroyed by fire.
The building was destroyed completely.

ALWAYS

Albert Ape is **always** friendly.
He is friendly at all times.
Night **always** follows day.

A.M.

This is the time from midnight to noon.
The new pupils will start school on Monday morning at
9 **a.m.**

AMAZE

Batty Bat can **amaze** his friends with his clever tricks. Batty Bat can surprise his friends with his clever tricks.
They wonder at his tricks.

AMBITION

[A]rnold Aircraft's **ambition** is to fly [ro]und the world.
[H]e hopes to fly round the world one [da]y soon.

AMBULANCE

[A]ndy **Ambulance** carries the sick [an]d injured to hospital as fast as he [ca]n.

AMONG

[Th]e children quarrelled **among** [th]emselves so the teacher divided the [sw]eets **among** the children.

AMUSE

[A]dam Apple can **amuse** his friends [by] rolling up and down the alley.
[Ev]eryone laughs at him.
[Th]ey all have fun.

ANCHOR

An **anchor** grips the sea bottom and so holds a ship in place.

ANCIENT

We saw the ruins of an **ancient** castle.
The castle is very old.
It was built nine hundred years ago.

AND

Annie
Antelope
and Albert
Ape are
good friends.
They like to
run **and**
jump **and**
play.

ANGEL

An **angel** is a messenger from God.
An **angel** is kind and good.

ANGLER

An **angler** is a person who fishes with a hook and a line.

ANGRY

My friend lost my favourite toy.
This made me very **angry**.
I was extremely annoyed.

ANIMAL

An **animal** is a creature that can feel and move. (A dog, a bird, a fish, a fly, a person and a worm are all **animals**.)
A plant is not an **animal**.

ANORAK

An **anorak** is a warm, waterproof jacket.

ANOTHER

Eat **another** sweet.
You may eat one more sweet.
Show me **another** kind of sweet.
I want a different kind of sweet.

ANSWER

Who can **answer** the question first?
The girl gave a quick **answer**.
When the telephone rings Polly Parrot will **answer** it.

ANT

An **ant** is a small insect.
Ants live together in large groups called colonies.

ANTELOPE

An **antelope** looks like a small deer with horns. **Antelope** chew the cud.

ANY

Choose **any** cake you like.
Have you **any** cream cakes?
No, we haven't **any**.

APARTMENT

Nice Nurse lives in an **apartment**.
Her flat has three cosy rooms.

APE

Apes are large monkeys that often live in trees.
Apes have no tails.
Albert **Ape** is a clever **ape**.

APEX

To reach the **apex** of a mountain you must climb to its highest point.
When you climb to the top of a mountain you have reached its **apex**.

APPLAUD

Albert Ape will **applaud** when Annie Antelope wins the race.
He will clap his hands.

APPLE

An **apple** is a kind of fruit and grows on **apple** trees.

An **apple** is good to eat.
Adam **Apple** is a rosy, red **apple**.

APPROVE

The teacher will **approve** of good work.
She will be pleased with good work.

APRICOT

An **apricot** is a pale, orange-coloured fruit. It is smaller than a peach.

APRIL

This is the fourth month of the year.
April has thirty days.
April comes after March.

APRON

An **apron** is a garment worn over our clothes to keep our clothes clean. Benjamin Butcher wears a striped **apron**

ARCH

An **arch** is curved.
Arches of wedge-shaped stone are often used to support bridges.
A rainbow **arches** across the sky.

ARMCHAIR

An **armchair** is a comfortable chair with side pieces to support your arms or elbows.

ARMY

An **army** is a group of soldiers trained to fight for their country in times of war.
An **army** of ants means a very large number of ants.

AROUND

Ally Alligator crawled **around** the big tree.
The tree measures two metres **around**.

ARROW

Robin Hood shot a silver **arrow** from his bow.

ARTIST

An **artist** paints pictures.
Albert Ape painted a picture. He is an **artist**.

AS

Sophie is **as** tall **as** James.
Sophie and James are equally tall.
As for the little boy, he is much smaller.

ASK

Ask Ally Alligator how old she is.
Ask Belinda Ballerina to dance.
Ask your friends to a party.
We **ask** a question and wait for an answer.

ASLEEP

Bouncing Baby is **asleep**.
He is not awake.
The tired baby fell **asleep**.

ASSEMBLY

We have **assembly** at school.
All the children meet in one room.

ASTONISH

The giant redwood trees of
California will **astonish** you.

They will surprise you.
They will fill you with wonder.

ASTROLOGY

People who believe in **astrology**
study the stars and planets to foretell
what will happen.

ASTRONAUT

An **astronaut** travels through outer
space in a
spacecraft.

AT

Jack is **at** home today.
He is in the house.
Jack goes to bed **at** nine o' clock.
When it is nine o' clock, he will go to
bed.

ATE

The children **ate** crisps and cake at
the party.
The horse **ate** the grass in his field.
The cat **ate** the fish in his dish.

ATHLETE

Frankie Frog is an **athlete**.
He can jump very high.
Ossie Ostrich is an **athlete**.
He can run very fast.

ATLAS

An **atlas** is a book of maps.
You will find a map of your country
in an **atlas**.

ATTACH

We are going to **attach** the tail to
our kite.
We shall
fasten the
tail to
the
kite.

ATTEMPT

Jack made an **attempt** to
climb the tree. He tried to climb it.

ATTENTION

The children were paying
attention to the teacher. They were
listening carefully.
The teacher called their **attention**
to the new dictionary.

ATTIC

The space just below the roof in a
house is called the **attic**.
People often store their old things in
the **attic**.

AUDIENCE

Our school play had a large **audience**
All the parents came to see it.

AUGUST

August is the eighth month of the year.
August has thirty-one days.

AUNT

My mother's sister is my **aunt**.
My father's sister is my **aunt**.
My uncle's wife is my **aunt**, too.

AUTHOR

An **author** is a person who writes books and stories.

AUTOMATIC

An **automatic** kettle turns itself off when the water has boiled.
An **automatic** washing machine will wash and rinse clothes by itself.

AUTUMN

A year is divided into four seasons.
Autumn is the season between summer and winter.

AVENUE

An **avenue** is a wide street with trees on both sides.
Rose lives on Park **Avenue**.

AVERAGE

Joe is an **average** boy.
He is like most boys.
An **average** day is an ordinary day when nothing special happens.

AVOID

Jenny has a cold.
She tries to **avoid** other people when she has a cold.
She stays away from them.

AWAKE

Bouncing Baby is wide **awake**.
He is not asleep.

AWAY

Father is **away** today.
He is not near.
The astronaut was far **away** from home.

AWFUL

There was an **awful** storm with thunder and lightning.
It was a dreadful storm.
Tom had an **awful** dream.
It was a very bad dream.

AXE

Farmer Brown chops wood with an **axe**.

Bb

BABY
A **baby** is a very young child.
Bouncing **Baby** is not very old.

BACK
Bertie Bear is riding on Hobby
Horse's **back**.
The **back** of something is the part
behind, like the **back** of this book.

BADGE
A **badge** is a small sign worn on
your clothes to show who you are or
to which group you belong.
Nice Nurse wears a **badge** on her
apron.

BADGER
Brock **Badger** lives in a cosy,
underground
burrow. He has
a white
face with
two
black
stripes.

BAG
We carry things in a **bag**. Daffy
Duck's friend carries her **handbag**
on her wing.

BAKER
Mother Goose likes to **bake** cakes.
She **bakes** cakes in an oven.
She is a good **baker**.

BALL

Clarence Cat loves to play with a
ball, especially a **ball** of wool!

BALLERINA

Belinda **Ballerina** dances in
a ballet.
Look at Elly Elephant, she thinks she
can dance on her toes too.

BALLOON
A **balloon** is
a small,
rubber
bag that
can be
filled with
air and used
as a toy. A
blown-up
balloon
can rise
and float in
the air.

BANANA
Mickey Monkey's favourite fruit is a
bright yellow **banana**.
Bananas grow in bunches
called hands.
Bananas grow in warm countries.

BAND
A **band** is a group of people.
Our school **band** plays music.
A narrow strip of cloth is also called
a **band**.
Benjamin Butcher has a red **band**
on his hat.

BANGLE
A **bangle** is a ring worn around
your wrist, arm or ankle.
Missy Mouse has a pretty **bangle**
on her wrist.

BARBEQUE
Piggles Pig is cooking his dinner on a **barbeque** outside in the open air.

BASKET
A **basket** is a container made of sticks or cane woven together. There is a **basket** of fruit on the table.

BAT
Batty **Bat** looks like a mouse with skin-like wings. He sleeps all day and flies at night. When we play baseball, cricket and rounders we strike or hit the ball with a wooden **bat**.

BAY
Bridlington has a lovely **bay**. A **bay** is a curved area of sheltered sea. Ships seek shelter in a **bay**.

BEACH
A **beach** is a seashore covered in sand or pebbles. We can build sandcastles on the **beach**.

BARBER
Barry **Barber's** business is cutting hair. He is trying to cut Dolly Donkey's tail but she keeps swishing it about.

BARGE
A **barge** is a large, flat-bottomed boat that sails on rivers and inland waterways.

BEAR
Bertie **Bear** is a large, furry animal with a very short tail. He likes to eat honey.

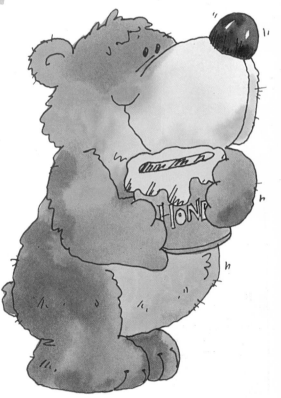

BARK
Digger Dog has a loud **bark**. He likes to **bark** at Clarence Cat.

BARREL
A **barrel** is a round container with flat ends. We store things in a **barrel**. The metal tube of a gun is called a **barrel**.

BATHROOM
Look at Peter Penguin having a bubble bath in the **bathroom**.

BEAUTIFUL
Belinda Ballerina is **beautiful**. She is very pretty.

BED

Gertie Goat is tired so she has gone to **bed** to have a rest.
We sleep in a **bed**.

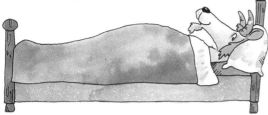

BEE

Guess who is making honey.
Yes, it is Buzzy **Bee**.
Watch out, he can sting too!

BEETLE

A **beetle** is a small insect with hard wing-cases.

BEFORE

You should wash your hands **before** you eat.
Two o' clock is earlier than four o' clock. It comes **before**.

BEHAVE

This is the way one acts.
Don't **behave** like a fool.
Act well and do what is right.

BEHIND

Dilly Deer is hiding **behind** a tree.
She is not in front of it.

BELIEVE

I **believe** what you say.
I think you are telling the truth.

BELL

A **bell** is a hollow, metal cup with a clapper that makes a ringing sound when we shake it.

BELONG

These seeds **belong** to Billy Budgie. They are his property. Does this book **belong** to you?
Do you own it?

BELOW

The basement is **below** the groun floor.
It is underneath it.
The ground is **below** the sky.
The sky is higher than the ground.

BELT

Chief Chef wears a **belt** around h waist to fasten his trousers.

BENCH

You may sit on a **bench** at your local park.
A **bench** is a long, hard seat, usually made of wood or stone.

BENEATH

Clarence Cat is sitting **beneath** the table.

He is sitting underneath the table.

BERTH

A **berth** is a built-up bed on a ship or a train.

Oh dear, Henry Hedgehog has fallen asleep in the Captain's **berth**.

BEST

Gertie Goat likes grass to eat **best** of all.

She prefers grass to any other food.
It is the **best** for her.

BET

I'll **bet** Annie Antelope can run faster than Tilly Tortoise.

Shall we have a **bet** on it?
Watch out, you may lose some money on the wager.

BETWEEN

Henrietta Hen walks **between** two rows of flowers.
She walks in the middle with a row on each side.
Naughty Henrietta!

BEYOND

The rainbow is **beyond** the mountains.
It is farther away than the mountains and is out of reach.

BIBLE

The **Bible** is a holy book consisting of the Old and New Testaments.

BICYCLE

Farmer Brown is riding his **bicycle**.
He is pedalling fast to catch Goosey Gander who has run away.

BIG

Elly Elephant is a **big** animal.
She is too large to get through the doorway.

BINOCULARS

Binoculars are special glasses with two eye-pieces for looking at things a long way off.

BIRD

A **bird** has two wings, feathers and a beak.
Carol Canary is a **songbird** with pretty, yellow feathers.
Most **birds** can fly.

BIRTH

Your date of **birth** is the day on which you were born.
This is your **birthday**.
When is your **birthday**?

BITE

Digger Dog does not **bite**.
He will not cut you with his teeth.

BITTER

Lemons are **bitter**.
They have a sharp, sour taste.
It is cold because there is a **bitter** wind.

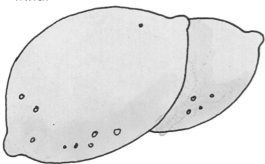

BLACK

Black is a colour.
Caw-Caw Crow has **black**, shiny feathers. You can see him flying round Farmer Brown's farm.

BLACKBOARD

Tommy Teacher uses chalk to write on the **blackboard** at school.

BLANKET

This is a thick, soft, cloth cover to keep us warm in bed in winter.
How many **blankets** do you have on your bed?

BLEED

Poor Dilly Deer, she has cut her nose on a prickly bush and made it **bleed**. Shall we send for Doc Doctor to stop the **bleeding**?

BLONDE

Aunty Ivy has **blonde** hair.
Her hair is light in colour.

BLOSSOM

A **blossom** is a flower, especially of a plant which produces fruit.

BLOT

A **blot** is a spot or stain usually made by a leaky pen.

BLOUSE

Dainty Doll is wearing a pink **blouse**.
A **blouse** is worn by a girl and covers the upper part of her body.

BLOW

Tommy Teacher will **blow** the whistle at the end of playtime.
You can also hear the wind **blow**.

BLUE

Blue is a colour. The sky is **blue**.
Billy Budgie's feathers are **blue** too.

BLUNT

When something is **blunt** it is not sharp.
A **blunt** or dull knife needs to be sharpened to make it cut properly.

BOARD

A **board** is a piece of long, thin, flat wood.

BOAT

A **boat** sails on water.
Flipper Fish has a red **boat**.
When he is tired of swimming around he sunbathes in his **boat**.

BODY

All the parts of a person or animal are its **body**.
Bertie Bear has a strong, healthy body.

BOOK

This dictionary is a **book**.
Do you like the pictures in this **book**?

BOOT

A **boot** is a shoe with tall sides to keep your feet warm and dry in bad weather.
Freddy Fox is proud of his new **boots**.

BORROW

Mickey Monkey wants to **borrow** some nuts from Squeaky Squirrel.
If you **borrow** something you must return it to the owner.

BOTH

Lucy Lamb has lost **both** her mittens. She has lost two mittens.

BOTTLE

A **bottle** is a narrow-necked, glass or plastic container for liquids.
Milk is delivered to your door in **bottles**.

BOTTOM

Captain Custard is searching for treasure at the **bottom** of the sea.
The **bottom** is the lowest part of anything.

BOUNCE

Can you **bounce** a ball?
Can you tap it and make it spring up and down?

BOWL

Digger Dog eats his dinner from a **bowl**. A **bowl** is a deep, round dish.

BOX

My favourite breakfast cereal comes in a **box**.
Aunty Ivy keeps her rings in a **jewel-box**.

BOY

Bouncing Baby is a **boy**.
He is a male child.
When he grows up he will be a man.

BRACELET

A **bracelet** is a piece of jewellery worn around the arm or wrist.

BRAIN

Your **brain** is in your head.
You think and feel with your **brain**.

BRAKE

Your bicycle has a **brake** on it to help you slow it down or stop it.
Whoosh! Minnie Mini-Bus's **brakes** are bad – she can't stop!

BRANCH

Olly Owl and Squeaky Squirrel are having a nap on a tree **branch**.
They are sitting on a limb of the tree.

BRASS

Some musical instruments are made of **brass** – a bright yellow metal.

BRAVE

Olly Owl is **brave**.
He is not afraid of the dark.
Policemen are **brave** too.

BREAD

Bread is made of flour, water, yeast and salt.
It is baked in an oven until it is golden brown.

BREAK

Oh dear, poor Spikey Spider!
How did he **break** a leg?
Never mind, he has seven left, he won't miss one!

BREAKFAST

This is the first meal of the day.
Your favourite **breakfast** cereal is in the box on the table.

BREATH

Take a deep **breath**.
Draw air into your lungs and now blow it out.
Your **breath** is the air you take in and let out.

BREATHE

We **breathe** by taking air into our lungs.
You should **breathe** through your nose.
You should take in air.

BREED

A **breed** is a type of animal.
A dachshund is a **breed** of dog.
Ally Alligator is a **breed** of reptile.

BREEZE

A **breeze** is a soft, gentle wind.
In winter it could be a very cold **breeze**.

BRICK

A **brick** is a block of clay used to build houses.
Piggles Pig made his house of **bricks**.

BRIDGE

A **bridge** is built to carry a road, railway or path across a river, road, ravine and so forth.
Bridges are used to cross over something.

BRIGHT

Leo Lion enjoys basking in the **bright** sunlight.
Leo is wearing a pair of **bright** red shorts.

BRING

Tommy Teacher wants you to **bring** a pet to school on Monday.
Whom will you **bring**?
Maybe I will **bring** Digger Dog.

BROAD

The Amazon is a **broad** river.
It is a very wide river.

BROKEN

Chief Chef has **broken** a glass.
He dropped the glass and it has **broken** into many pieces.

BROOK

A **brook** is a small stream.
Sometimes there are lots of fish in a **brook**.

BROTHER

My **brother**, John, and I have the same parents.
John is Jane's **brother**.

BROUGHT

Look what Henrietta Hen has **brought** for her chicks.
She has come with some corn for their supper.

BROWN

Bertie Bear's coat is **brown**.
Brown is a colour.
Chocolates are usually **brown** in colour.

BRUISE

Daniel Dwarf has banged his knee.
He has a **bruise** on his knee.
The **bruise** on his knee turned black and blue.

BRUSH

You should always **brush** your teeth after eating food.
You clean your teeth with a **toothbrush**.
You **brush** your hair with a **hairbrush**.

BUCKET

Jack and Jill used a **bucket** to carry water.

BUCKLE

There will be a **buckle** on your belt. It is a type of fastener for joining two straps together.

BUD

A **bud** is a flower or leaf before it opens.
This is a **rose-bud**.
There are **buds** on the trees too.

BUDGERIGAR

Billy is a **budgerigar**.
He lives in a lovely cage and sometimes he talks.
Billy **Budgie** is a small, brightly-coloured bird.

BUILD

Hobby Horse needs a new stable.
Will you help to **build** it?
Will you help to make it?
But first, shall we ask Bully Bulldozer to clear the site?

BULLDOZER

Bully **Bulldozer** is a strong tractor with a big blade in front.
He pushes soil and other things.

BUN

A **bun** is a small round cake. Would you like to taste one of Mother Goose's **buns**.

BUNCH

Bananas grow in a **bunch**.
Mickey Monkey has a **bunch** of bananas in his hand.

BUNDLE

A **bundle** is a number of things fastened together.
Brock Badger collects sticks and ties them into a **bundle** with a piece of string.

BURN

Do not touch the hot plate, you will **burn** your hand.
If you stand too near the fire it will **burn** you.

BURY

Digger Dog likes to **bury** his bones.
He digs a hole in the garden and hides them.

BUS

People ride in a **bus**.
Big **Bus** stops at a **bus-stop** and picks up passengers.
He is bigger than a car.

BUSH

A **bush** is a small, low tree.
Roses grow on a **bush**.

BUSY

Mother Goose is always **busy**.
She is always working.
She is **busy** all day long.

BUT

But means except or yet.
Daffy Duck's friend loves to swim in the pond **but** Clarence Cat does not like the water.

BUTCHER

Benjamin **Butcher** sells meat at the market. We buy meat from a **butcher**.

BUTTER

This is the yellow fat made from cream.
We put **butter** on our bread to make it taste good.

BUTTON

Aunty Ivy has to sew a **button** on Belinda Ballerina's dress.
Buttons are fasteners.

BUY

We go to the shop to **buy** sweets.
We **buy** things with money.

BUZZ

We hear a **buzz** when **Buzzy** Bee flies to his hive.
He makes a low, humming sound.

BY

By means using or near.
We go to school **by** bus.
Big Bus takes us to school which is **by** the Town Hall.
You can sit **by** me.
You can sit near me.

Cc

CABBAGE

This is a round-shaped vegetable.
Curly **Cabbage** is a green **cabbage**.
Sometimes we eat **cabbage** with our roast beef.

CAKE

Cake is a sweet food baked in the oven.
If you are lucky you will have a birthday **cake** on your birthday.

CALENDAR

A **calendar** lists the months, weeks and days of the year.
A **calendar** shows the day of the week on which each day of the month falls.

CALF

Cassy **Calf** is a baby cow.
She is the daughter of Camilla Cow.

CAMERA

We take photographs with a **camera**.
Bobby Boy's **camera** takes good pictures.

CANARY

Carol **Canary** is a pretty, yellow bird who sings sweetly.
She is Bobby Boy's pet.

CANDLE

A **candle** gives light. It is made of **candle** wax.
When I was one year old I had one **candle** on my birthday cake.

CANNOT

Polly Parrot **cannot** swim.
She is unable to swim.
Clarence Cat can climb the tree but Digger Dog **cannot** climb the tree.

CANOE

A **canoe** is a small, light boat that is propelled by paddles.

CANVAS

Canvas is a heavy, coarse cloth.
Canvas is used for tents and sails and oil paintings.

CAP

Tiggy Tiger likes to wear a **cap** on his head.
A **cap** is a soft hat with a peak at the front which keeps his head warm in cold weather.

CAPITAL

London is the **capital** of England.
Rome is the **capital** of Italy.
A **capital** is the most important city of a country.
What is the **capital** of France?

CAPTAIN

Captain Custard is the person in charge of the ship.
He is the leader.
Johnny is the **captain** of our football team.

CAR

Daddy has a **car**.
A **car** is a motor vehicle.
Sometimes when it is raining he takes me to school in the **car**.

CARAVAN

A **caravan** is a house on wheels which can be pulled by a car or a horse.

CAROL

A **carol** is a religious song sung at Christmas.
Which is your favourite **carol**?

CARPENTER

A **carpenter** makes things out of wood.
A **carpenter** also repairs broken wooden objects.

CARPET

A **carpet** is a piece of thick, woven material used to cover a floor.
Mother has a nice, blue **carpet** in the bathroom.

CARROT

A **carrot** is an orange-coloured vegetable.
Dolly Donkey loves to eat **carrots**.
They are her favourite food.

CARRY

When you **carry** something you take it from one place to another.
You **carry** your homework home from school.

CARTOON

A **cartoon** is a funny drawing or a film. Most children like to watch **cartoon** films on TV.

CASH

Coins and paper money are called **cash**.
You can put **cash** into your piggy-bank to keep it safe.

CASHIER

This is the person in charge of cash at a bank or office.
Cashiers keep an account of all the money they handle.

CASTLE

Kings and Queens live in **castles**.
Castles are large, strong buildings with thick walls and towers.

CAT

Clarence is a naughty **cat**.
Whoops! He's trying to catch Gilly Goldfish.

CATAMARAN

A **catamaran** is a kind of boat with two hulls which are joined together in the middle.

CATCH

Clarence Cat is still trying to **catch** Gilly Goldfish.
I hope he does not get hold of her.

CATERPILLAR

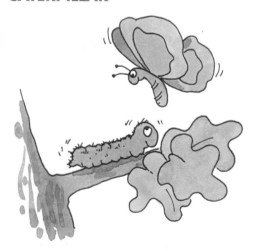

A **caterpillar** looks like a furry worm.
When it grows up it becomes a moth or a butterfly.

CAVE

A **cave** is a deep hole in the side of a hill or cliff.

CENTRE

There are two holes near the **centre** of a button.
They are in the middle of the button.
The **centre** of something is the middle.

CEREAL

Cereal is a breakfast food made from grain crops such as wheat, rice or maize.
Henrietta Hen likes to eat **cereals**.

CHAIN

Digger Dog has a **chain** around his neck.
A **chain** is a string of metal rings joined together.

CHAIR

A **chair** is something we sit on. Bouncing Baby sits in a **high-chair** to eat his meals.

CHALK

Tommy Teacher writes on the blackboard with **chalk**.
Chalk is a stick of soft rock with which to write.

CHALLENGE

Tilly Tortoise said to the hare, "I **challenge** you to a race!"
Tilly thought she could beat the hare because in the fable by Aesop the tortoise beat the hare.
Do you know the story?

CHAPTER

A **chapter** is part of a book.
Each section of this book is a **chapter**.
This 'C' section is a **chapter**.

CHART

A **chart** is a special kind of map. Sailors use **charts** to navigate. The weatherman looks at a weather **chart** to tell us about the weather.

CHEAP

Cheap things do not cost a lot of money.
They are low in price.
They are not dear.

CHEAT

You must not **cheat**.
You must always be honest in your work or play.
Nobody likes to play games with someone who **cheats**.

CHEEK

This is the side of your face.
Cheeks are the fleshy parts on either side of your face under your eyes. Bouncing Baby has dimples in his **cheeks**.

CHEESE

This is a savoury food made from milk.
Missy Mouse likes to eat **cheese**.

CHEF

Chief **Chef** is a cook.
He is the head cook at the school.
He is the person in charge of cooking.

CHERRY

A **cherry** is a small, round fruit with a stone in the middle.
Cherries grow on **cherry** trees and most **cherries** are red.

CHESS

Chess is a game for two players with 16 **chessmen** each.
It is played on a black and white, chequered board with 64 squares.
Can you play **chess**?
Maybe Daddy can teach you.

CHEW

We crush food with our teeth when we **chew**.
Digger Dog likes to **chew** a bone.
Bouncing Baby cannot **chew** because he has no teeth.

CHICKEN

A **chicken** is a young bird (fowl).
Chickens usually live on farms.
Charlie is a **chicken**.

CHILD

Bobby Boy is a **child**.
He is a young person.
You are a **child**.
When you grow up you will be an adult.

CHIMNEY

A **chimney** is a hollow, upright passage that carries smoke away from a fireplace.
The smoke goes up the **chimney**.

CHIMPANZEE

Champ Chimp is a **chimpanzee**. He is related to Mickey Monkey and Guy Gorilla.

CHOCOLATE

This can be a sweet or a bedtime drink.

Chocolate is made from the roasted beans of the cacao tree.

CHOOSE

Daffy Duck must **choose** which hat to wear today.
I think she will pick a red one.
She will **choose** a red one.

CHORUS

Do you sing in the school **chorus**?
A **chorus** can be a group of singers or dancers.

CHRISTMAS

Christmas comes once a year on December 25th.
Jesus Christ was born on **Christmas** Day.

CHURCH

A **church** is a building where we worship God.

CINEMA

We go to the **cinema** to watch films in public.
It is usually a large building with rows of seats which all face a big screen.

CIRCLE

This is a **circle**.
It is a perfectly round ring.

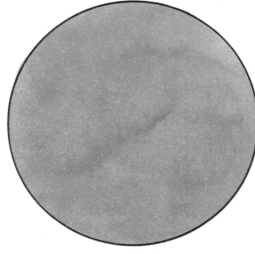

CIRCUS

A **circus** is a travelling show with lots of animals, clowns and acroba[t]
The show is performed inside a ver[y] big tent called a big top.

CITIZEN

You are a **citizen** of this country.
You live in this country.

CLAP

We **clap** when we hit our hands together.
Clap your hands and sing along with Carol Canary.

CLASS

Tommy Teacher is showing the **clas**[s] how to write on the blackboard.
A **class** is a group of children or adults who are taught together.

30

CLAW

Tiggy Tiger has sharp **claws**.
They are the pointed parts of his paws, like the nails on our hands.
Clarence Cat has sharp **claws** too.

CLEAN

We must **clean** our teeth after eating food.
To be **clean** is to be well-washed.
Albert Ape's jeans are dirty. They are not **clean**.

CLEAR

It is a **clear** day today.
There are no clouds in the sky.

CLEVER

This boy is **clever**.
He got all his sums right at school today.

CLIFF

A **cliff** is a high, steep rock face near the sea.
Do not go near the edge.
It can be dangerous.

CLIMB

Watch Clarence Cat, he is trying to **climb** the tree.
Watch him go up the tree.

CLOCK

We look at a **clock** to see what time it is.
What time does this **clock** say?

CLOSED

The Post Office is **closed** on Sundays.
It does not open on Sundays.
When the door is **closed** we cannot go inside.

CLOTHES

We wear **clothes** on our bodies.
I think Elly Elephant needs a new skirt.
She has grown too big for her **clothes**.

CLOWN

A **clown** is the funny person who makes you laugh at a circus.
Sometimes Mickey Monkey acts like a **clown**.
He fools about.

COACH

A **coach** is a bus.
A **coach** is also someone who teaches, usually a sport.
Tommy Teacher is a **coach**.

COAL

Coal is a fuel.
It is hard and black and is dug from the ground.
We burn **coal** in a fireplace to heat the room.

COAT

It is cold outside.
Put on your **coat** to keep warm.
When an animal has beautiful fur,
we say it has a beautiful **coat**.

COBWEB

Spikey Spider spins a silken
cobweb to catch flies. It is made of
sticky thread.

COCONUT

A **coconut** is a large, hairy nut that
grows on palm trees.
The centre is filled with milky juice.

COIN

This is a piece of money made
of metal.
How many **coins** do you have in
your piggy bank?

COLD

The weather is **cold** today.
You must put your coat on before
going outside.
When it is not warm it is **cold**.

COLLAR

The **collar** on this shirt is white.
It is a stiff band that goes around
the neck.
Digger Dog wears a **collar** round
his neck.

COLLEGE

If you work well at school you may
choose to go to **college** when you
are older.
It is a place where people study
when they leave school.

COLOUR

Red, yellow, blue, green and purple
are all **colours**.
What **colour** is Carol Canary?

COLT

A young, male horse is a **colt**,
whereas a young, female horse is
called a filly.

COMB

Hobby Horse's mane is tangled.
You must **comb** it with a **comb** to
take out the tangles.

COMIC

An amusing comedian is a **comic**.
He tells funny stories.
It is also a magazine for children.
Which is your favourite **comic**?

COMPASS

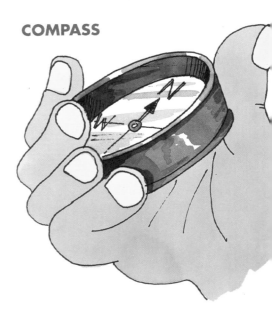

A **compass** is an instrument for
showing directions.
The needle of a **compass** always
points to the magnetic north pole.

COMPUTER

A **computer** is an electronic machine that stores and processes large amounts of information at great speed.

CONDUCTOR

A **conductor** is the leader of a band.
A bus **conductor** collects fares.

CONTINENT

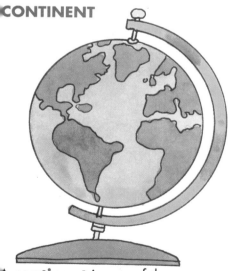

A **continent** is one of the seven great masses of land on the earth's surface.
Africa, Asia, Australia, North America, South America, Europe and Antarctica are their names.

CONTINUE

To go on is to **continue** doing something.
Shall we **continue** reading this book?

COPY

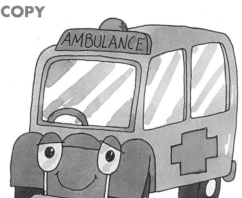

Can you **copy** this picture of Andy Ambulance?
Can you make a picture that looks the same?

CORNER

Little Jack Horner sat in the **corner**.
A **corner** can be where two streets meet.

CORRECT

To **correct** mistakes is to make right the errors.
Tommy Teacher has to **correct** your homework.

CORRIDOR

This is a long, narrow passage off which rooms open.
There will be several **corridors** at your school.
You must not run down a **corridor**.

COST

The **cost** is the price paid for something.
Do you know the **cost** of this book?

COTTAGE

A **cottage** is a small house.
Mother Goose lives in a thatched **cottage**.

COTTON

Cotton is a soft, white, woolly substance that can be used to make thread.
It comes from the **cotton** bush which grows in warm areas.
Belinda Ballerina's dress is made of **cotton**.

COUNT

To **count** is to add up.
Can you **count** from 1 to 100?
Can you say the numbers in order?
You can **count** on me means you can rely on me.

COUNTRY

Farmer Brown lives in the **country** not the town.

COUSIN

Your **cousin** is the child of your aunt or uncle.
Jane and Jill are **cousins**.

COVER

Please **cover** Bouncing Baby with a blanket.

Please put a blanket over him to keep him warm.

COW

Camilla is a **cow**.
We get milk from a **cow**.

COWBOY

A **cowboy** rides a horse and looks after cattle on a ranch.
There are many **cowboys** in America.

CRAB

A **crab** is a type of shellfish with eight legs and two claws.

CRASH

What a **crash**!
What a loud noise!
Tracy Train has **crashed** into the buffers at the station.

CRAYON

This is a coloured wax-stick or coloured pencil.
We colour pictures with **crayons**.
Can you **crayon** a colourful picture for Mummy?

CREAM

We get **cream** from the milk of Camilla Cow.
Cream is also used to make butter and is a pale yellow colour.

CROCODILE

Christopher **Crocodile** is a large river animal with a long nose, a thick skin, big teeth and short legs.

CROSSING

There is a **crossing** outside your school so that you can **cross** the road safely.

CROW

Caw-Caw **Crow** is a large bird with shiny, black feathers.

He has a loud, harsh voice that says "Caw! Caw!"

CROWN

On important occasions the Queen wears a **crown** on her head.
It is a circle of gold with jewels round it.

CRY

Bouncing Baby is **crying** because he is hungry.
We shed tears when we **cry**.

CUCUMBER

A **cucumber** is a long, green vegetable, usually eaten raw with a salad.

CUPBOARD

This is a piece of furniture with shelves inside on which to store things.
Mummy keeps cereals in a **cupboard**.

CURRENT

A **current** is a flow of air or water.
The river has a rapid **current**.
A **current** is also a flow of electricity through a wire.

CURTAINS

We hang **curtains** at our windows.
The **curtains** at a theatre are wide enough to go across the whole stage.
Curtains are usually made of cloth.

CURVE

A **curve** is not straight.
There is a **curve** in the road.
There is a bend in the road.

CUSHION

This is a soft pillow on which you can sit.
A **cushion** in a chair makes it more comfortable.

CUSTOMER

A **customer** is the person who buys something from a shop.
Benjamin Butcher is telling a **customer** how good the beef is today.

CUT

Bouncing Baby has **cut** a new tooth.
A new tooth has come out through his gum.
A **cut** is also a small wound.
We **cut** things into pieces with a

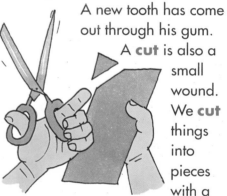

pair of scissors, a knife or a saw.

CUTLERY

We eat our food with **cutlery**.
Knives, forks and spoons are **cutlery**.

CYCLE

Farmer Brown will **cycle** after Goosey Gander.
He will ride his bicycle as fast as he can to catch naughty Goosey Gander.

Dd

DAD

Dad is the name for father.
I call my father **Dad**.
Sometimes I call him **Daddy**.

DAFFODIL

A **daffodil** is a plant with a yellow, trumpet-shaped flower and long, slender leaves.
Dainty Doll dances around a clump of **daffodils**.

DANGER

Beware! If you are in **danger** you may get hurt.
When the light for the traffic is red, and the traffic has stopped, we can cross the street without **danger**.

DARK

At night the sky is **dark**.
At night the sky is not light.
Clouds and rain make a **dark** and gloomy day.

DATE

Look at the calendar and find the **date** of your birthday. The number on a coin is the **date** it was made.

DAUGHTER

A girl is the **daughter** of her mother and father.
Goosey Gander has a **daughter** called Gracie Gosling.

DAY

A **day** is divided into 24 hours.
There are 7 **days** in a week.
The first **day** of the week is Sunday.

DEAR

Goosey Gander's daughter is very **dear** to him.
He loves her very much.
The coat is very **dear**.
It costs a lot of money.

DECEMBER

This is the twelfth and last month of the year.
The date of Christmas Day is **December** 25th.

DEER

Dilly **Deer** is a graceful, wild animal.
A father **deer** is called a buck.
A mother **deer** is called a doe.
A baby **deer** is called a fawn.

DELIVER

The postman **delivers** letters to our houses.
He brings letters to our houses.
Eddy Eagle will **deliver** his party invitations.
He will give them out.

DESCRIBE

Will you **describe** your holiday?
Will you tell me about your holiday?

DESK

A **desk** is a table at which we can write, read and draw. It often has drawers in which paper can be kept. Daniel Dwarf is sitting at his **desk** reading his dictionary.

DESSERT

We eat **dessert** at the end of a meal.
Would you like apple pie, fruit or ice-cream for **dessert**?

DEW

Dew is formed at night on the cool grass.
The grass had small drops of water on it this morning.

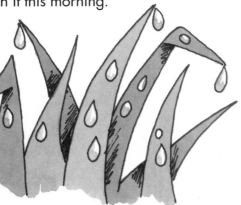

DIARY

Bobby Boy writes things in his **diary**.
Doc Doctor has a large **diary** in which he keeps a daily record of his work.

DICTIONARY

A **dictionary** is a book of words from A to Z in alphabetical order.
This book is a **dictionary**.
A **dictionary** tells us the meaning of words.

DIFFERENT

Timmy Tank is **different** from Andy Ambulance.
The two vehicles are not the same.
They are not alike.

DIFFICULT

This trick is **difficult**.
It is hard to do.

DIG

Digger Dog will **dig** a hole with his claws.
He likes to **dig** deep holes to bury his bones.

DINNER

Dinner is our main meal of the day.
At our house we have **dinner** at six o'clock in the evening.

DINOSAUR

A **dinosaur** is one of a group of extinct reptiles.
Some **dinosaurs** were bigger than Elly Elephant and some **dinosaurs** were smaller than Clarence Cat.

DIRECTION

In which **direction** did Arnold Aircraft go?
Did he go north, south, east or west?

DIRTY

Mickey Monkey washed his hands because they were **dirty**.
His hands were not clean.

DISAPPEAR

The sun will **disappear** behind a cloud.
It will go out of sight.
You will not be able to see it.

DISH

A **dish** is something we use to hold food.
We eat from **dishes**. Cups, saucers, plates and bowls are **dishes**.

DIVIDE

Tommy Teacher will **divide** the sweets between the children.
He will share the sweets between them.
They will each get some sweets.

DO

Do your work well.
Your teacher will be pleased if you **do** your best.
When you **do** something you carry out some action or task.

DOCTOR

A **doctor** is a person who takes care of your health.
A **doctor** knows how to treat diseases.
When I am ill **Doc Doctor** comes to examine me.

DOG

A **dog** is an animal.
Digger is a pet **dog**.
Digger is a clever **dog**.
He can do difficult tricks.

DOLL

A **doll** is a toy.
Dainty **Doll** looks just like a little girl.

DONKEY

A **donkey** is an animal that looks like a small horse.
A **donkey** has long ears and a tuft of hair at the end of its tail.
Dolly **Donkey** says, "Hee-Haw."

DOOR

A **door** opens or closes the entrance to a building or a room.
Dad opened the front **door**.

DOT

A **dot** is a small round spot.
At the end of this sentence there is a **dot**.
There are blue **dots** on Dainty Doll's dress.

DOUBLE

To **double** is to make two of something.
John's cake is **double** the size of mine.
If a person looks just like you we say he is your **double**.

DOUBT

I **doubt** Jim's story.
I am not sure it is true.

DOUGHNUT

A **doughnut** is a round, fried cake, sometimes with a hole in its centre.

DOWN

To go **down** means to go from a higher place to a lower place.
The children ran **down** from the top of the hill.

DRAW

This boy likes to **draw**.
He will **draw** a horse.
He will make a picture of a horse.
He will **draw** the picture with a pencil.

DREAM

A **dream** is something imagined during sleep.
Jolly Elephant had a lovely **dream**.
In her **dream** she was dancing in the ballet with Belinda Ballerina.

DRESS

Dainty Doll wears a polka-dot **dress**.
Belinda Ballerina wears a **dress** too.
I can **dress** myself means I can put my clothes on.

DRILL

A **drill** is a tool which makes holes in wood or metal.
To **drill** is to practise. When we have a fire **drill** we practise how to get out of the building.

DRINK

When we **drink** we swallow a liquid.
Watch Bouncing Baby **drink** his milk.
We **drink** when we are thirsty.

DRIP

To **drip** means to fall in drops.
Rain **drips** from the trees.
Water was **dripping** from the tap.
The spilt lemonade **dripped** from the edge of the table.

DRIVE

Farmer Brown can **drive** the tractor.
He can make the tractor go.
Father will **drive** the nail in.
He will hammer the nail into the wood.

DROP

A **drop** is a small amount of liquid in a round shape.
A **drop** of rain fell on my nose.
To **drop** something is to let it fall.

DROWN

If you go into deep water you may **drown**.
If you are under water and cannot breathe you will die.

DRUM

A **drum** is a musical instrument.
Bouncing Baby beats his **drum** with his hands.
Baby Brother beats his **drum** with sticks.

DRY

When something is **dry** it is not wet.
Dust is **dry**.
After washing our hands we **dry** them with a towel.
We wipe off the water.

DUCK

A **duck** is a common water bird which has a wide bill and a short neck.
Daffy **Duck** says, "Quack! Quack!" as she waddles along on her short legs.

DUE

Arnold Aircraft is **due** at midnight.
He is expected to arrive at midnight.
The train is **due** at noon.
It should come at noon.

DULL

The knife is **dull**.
It is not sharp.
Yesterday was a **dull** day.
It was not clear and bright.

DUMB

The teddy bear is **dumb**.
He is not able to speak.

DUMP

The men **dump** the rubbish into the big truck.
The rubbish will be taken to a **dump** to be burned.

DURING

Bouncing Baby slept **during** the storm.
He slept while it was going on.

DUST

The rug is full of **dust**.
It is full of tiny bits of dirt.
Buzzy Bee is covered with pollen, the yellow **dust** from flowers.

DUTY

A **duty** is an action one ought to do.
Feeding Clarence Cat is Bobby Boy's **duty**.
He has been given that task to do.

DWARF

A **dwarf** is a very small person.
In this book Daniel **Dwarf** is a kind, little man with magic power.

DWELL

Where do you **dwell**?
Where do you live?
Camilla Cow and Cassie Calf **dwell** in the countryside.
They live in the countryside.

DYE

Belinda Ballerina's pink dress is faded.
She can **dye** it red.
She can soak it in **dye** to change the colour.

Ee

EACH

The clown gave **each** of the children a balloon.
He gave every child a balloon.

EAGLE

Eddy **Eagle** is a large bird. He has sharp claws called talons. He sees a long way with his sharp eyes.

EAR

The **ear** is the part of the body used for hearing. Dolly Donkey has long, furry **ears**.
An **ear** is also the word for the seeds at the top of a stalk of corn or wheat.

EARLY

Albert Ape awoke **early** this morning.
He is going to Bertie Bear's birthday party. He will arrive before the other guests. He will be **early**.

EARTH

Our world is called the **earth**.
The **earth** in Digger Dog's garden is good, soft soil. It was easy for him to bury his bones in the **earth**.

EAST

Arnold Aircraft flew towards the **east**. He flew in the direction of the sunrise. The sun rises in the **east** and sets in the west.

EASY

The puzzle is **easy** to do. It is not hard to do.
This dictionary is **easy** to understand. It is not difficult.

EAT

When we **eat** we chew and swallow food.
Would you care for something to **eat**?
Camilla Cow and Oscar Ox **eat** grass and grain.

EGG

An **egg** is an oval object laid by birds and some animals.
We eat hens' **eggs**.
Birds, fish, insects, snakes and alligators are born from **eggs**.

EIGHT

Eight is one more than seven.
When you add 4 and 4 you have **8**.
Spikey Spider has **eight** legs.

EIGHTEEN

Eighteen is eight more than ten.
10 and 8 are **18**.
When you add 6 and 6 and 6 you have **18**.

ELBOW

An **elbow** is a joint.
We bend our arms at our **elbows**.

ELECTRIC

Things that use **electricity** to work are called **electric** The **electric** light bulb uses **electricity** Mother Goose bakes cakes in an **electric** oven.

ELEPHANT

Elly **Elephant** is very large and very strong. She has a thick skin and a long trunk to pick up food and water.

ELEVEN

Eleven is one more than ten. When you add 10 and 1 you have **11** There are **eleven** players in a soccer team.

ELF

Eric **Elf** is not a real person. He is a kind of fairy who is very tiny and full of mischief.

ELSE

Bobby Boy is ill so you must invite someone **else** to the party. Will somebody **else** come? Snowy Snail will come instead of Bobby. Hurry, Snowy, or **else** you will be late!

EMPLOY

Chief Chef is **employed** to cook meals. He is paid to do this work.

EMPTY

Daffy Duck's handbag is **empty**. There is nothing in it. Bouncing Baby drank all his milk and his bottle is **empty** now.

END

The 'Z' chapter is at the **end** of this book. It is the last part of the dictionary. The party will **end** at five o'clock. The party will finish at five o'clock.

ENEMY

A soldier fights the **enemy**. He fights the people who are against him. Eric Elf is my friend. He is not my **enemy**. He does not want to hurt me.

ENERGY

Mickey Monkey is so full of **energy** that he cannot keep still. Mother Goose has lots of **energy** too; she is always working.

ENGINE

An **engine** is a machine that makes things work. Bully Bulldozer has an **engine** to make him move. A large **engine** pulls Tracy Train.

ENJOY

Mickey Monkey and Albert Ape **enjoy** parties. They have a good time at parties. Did you **enjoy** the cartoon? Did you like it? Did the cartoon make you happy?

ENOUGH

[B]obby Boy ate two ice creams but [d]oes not want any more – he has [e]aten **enough**

[M]elinda Ballerina has **enough** [ri]bbon to make two bows for her [h]air.

[E]NTER

[T]his means to go in somewhere. The [ch]ildren **enter** the classroom at nine [o']clock. Tommy Teacher says, "You [m]ay **enter** now. You may come in."

[E]NTERTAIN

[Ne]lly Elephant likes to [e]ntertain us [at] the circus. [Sh]e amuses [us] with her [cl]ever [tr]icks.

[E]NTRANCE

[Th]e **entrance** is the way to go in. [Th]e boy will enter the park by the [bi]g gates at the **entrance**.

ENVELOPE

An **envelope** is a paper cover for a letter, or papers, to be sent in the post. On the front of the **envelope** we write the name and address of the person to whom we are writing.

EQUAL

We use this word to describe things that are the same in amount, size or value.
The children had **equal** shares of the birthday cake.
A square has four **equal** sides. The sides are all the same.

EQUATOR

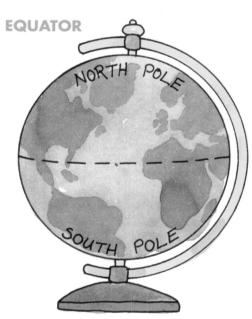

The **equator** is an imaginary line around the middle of the earth, halfway between the North Pole and the South Pole.

ERASE

Tommy Teacher will **erase** the writing from the blackboard. He will rub it out with a cloth **eraser**.
We use a rubber **eraser** to **erase** pencil marks.

ERROR

An **error** is a mistake. Something which has been done incorrectly is an **error**. Tommy Teacher found two **errors** in Bobby Boy's homework.

ESCALATOR

An **escalator** is a moving staircase. At the department store there are a lot of **escalators** going up and down.

ESCAPE

Billy Budgie cannot **escape** from his cage. He cannot get out of the cage to freedom.

ESSENTIAL

Food, air and water are **essential** to enable us to stay alive. We must have all three to stay alive.

EVEN

Even means equal or level or smooth.

This road is **even**; there are no hills. The **even** numbers can be exactly divided by two. 2, 4, 6, 8, 10 are **even** numbers.

EVENING

This is the end of the day between sunset and bedtime. Baby Brother goes to bed early in the **evening**.

EVENT

An **event** is something that happens or takes place. Bouncing Baby's party is a happy **event**.

EVERY

Every raindrop is wet. All raindrops are wet. **Every** bird has feathers. Each one has feathers.

EVIL

Evil things are bad, wrong and harmful. **Evil** witches cast wicked spells in fairy stories.

EXACT

Exact means without any error whatsoever. Did you make an **exact** copy of Andy Ambulance? Was it absolutely correct in every detail?

EXAMINATION

Bobby Boy is ill with a cold. Doc Doctor made a careful **examination** of his throat and ears. Tommy Teacher gave the children an **examination** in mathematics. They thought the test was easy to do.

EXCELLENT

The children's examination results were **excellent**. They were <u>very</u>, <u>very</u> good. Mother Goose bakes **excellent** cakes.

EXCEPT

Chief Chef works every day **except** Sunday. He has a holiday on Sunday.

EXCHANGE

Tommy Teacher asked two girls to **exchange** places. He asked them to change places with each other. We **exchange** presents with our friends at Christmas.

EXCITED

Daffy Duck and Lucy Lamb are **excited** about the visit to the circus. They are filled with delight at the thought of it.

EXCUSE

Snowy Snail has a good **excuse** for arriving late. "Please **excuse** me," he says. "I'm sorry, but I cannot move any faster."

44

EXERCISE

We need **exercise** to keep our bodies and minds healthy. When we run we **exercise** our legs. Swimming is an excellent form of **exercise**.

EXHAUSTED

Goosey Gander was **exhausted** after running from Farmer Brown. He was tired out so he went to bed early.

EXIT

The **exit** is the way to go out. Tommy Teacher's school has seven **exits**.

EXPAND

A balloon will **expand** if it is filled with air. It will get bigger.

EXPECT

We **expect** sunny days in summer. When the clouds become dark we **expect** rain. We think that it will happen.

EXPENSIVE

Belinda Ballerina has a very **expensive** dress. It cost a lot of money.

EXPLAIN

I do not know this word. The dictionary will **explain** it. The dictionary will tell what the word means.

EXPLODE

The firework will **explode**. It will break into pieces with a loud bang. Fireworks must be treated with care because they **explode**.

EXPRESS

Baby Brother tried to **express** his idea clearly. He tried to tell us so that we could understand it. An **express** train is a very fast train.

EXTEND

We **extend** our hands. We hold them out to shake hands with our friends. If we **extend** something, we make it longer.

EXTRA

This means more than you would normally need or have. Bobby Boy had an **extra** ice-cream. Tommy Teacher gave the children **extra** time to finish their work.

EYE

An **eye** is the part of the body with which we see. We have two **eyes**. The hole in a needle and the little spots on potatoes are called **eyes**.

Ff

FACE
The front part of your head is your **face**.
Felicity Fairy has a pretty **face**

FACT
A **fact** is something that is known to be true or to have happened.
It is a **fact** that birds lay eggs.
It is a **fact** that Columbus discovered America in 1492.

FACTORY
A **factory** is a building in which things are made, usually with the help of machines and special tools.
Cars are made in a **factory**.

FADE
When something **fades** it loses its colour or brightness. Washing made Belinda Ballerina's dress **fade**.
When the sun sets, daylight will **fade**.

FAIL
If you **fail** to do something you do not succeed. You are not able to do it.
Elly Elephant will try to dance on her toes but I think she will **fail**.

FAIR
Dainty Doll has **fair** hair. She has light-coloured hair.
The weather is **fair** today. It is clear and sunny.
A **fair** is where people go to show and sell things.

FAIRY
A **fairy** is a tiny, make-believe person in stories. Felicity is a good **fairy** and uses her magic to help human beings.

FALL
To **fall** means to drop or come down.
Leaves **fall** from trees.
Hold Bouncing Baby's hand and do not let him **fall**.
Poor Humpty Dumpty had a great **fall**!

FALSE
This means not true or not real.
Bobby Boy wears a **false** face on Hallowe'en. He wears a mask to disguise himself.
Circus clowns often wear **false** noses.

FAMILY
A father and mother and their children are a **family**
Bouncing Baby is the youngest member of his **family**

FAMINE
The country had a **famine** and there was little food for the people.
Many people died during the **famine** in Ethiopia.

FAMOUS
Arnold Aircraft will be **famous** once he has flown around the world
He will be very well-known.

FAN

A **fan** is something used to stir the air and cool us.
Natalie Niece waves a paper **fan** to cool her face.
Dad cools the room with an electric **fan**

FAR

Arnold Aircraft has flown **far** away. He is not near; he is a long way off.
Eddie Eagle can see **far**.
Dad's hat is **far** too big for me. It is much too big for me.

FARE

A **fare** is the money we pay to ride in a public vehicle.
A taxicab has a meter for recording the **fare**

FAREWELL

We gave Uncle Harry a **farewell** party. He is going on a trip. We said goodbye and wished him good luck.

FARM

A **farm** is the land a farmer has on which to raise crops or animals. A **farm** is where our food is grown. A **farm** usually has buildings where animals are kept.

FARMER

Farmer Brown owns a farm. He works on the farm and grows vegetables and corn. He raises sheep and cattle too and milks his cows twice a day.

FASHION

Fashion is a style of dress or behaviour that most people like and try to copy.

FAST

One-two-three-go! Run as **fast** as you can.
Can you run as **fast** as Annie Antelope?

FAT

Fat is a food. **Fat** is found in **fat** meat, milk, butter, and other foods. Doughnuts are fried in hot **fat**. Piggles Pig and Elly Elephant are **fat**; their bodies are plump and round.

FATHER

I call my **father** Dad. I am my **father's** child. I am also my mother's child. My **father** and mother are my parents.
A **father** is the male parent.

FAULT

The milk spilled but it was not Bouncing Baby's **fault**. He was not to blame.
Tommy Teacher found **fault** with Bobby Boy's homework. He found mistakes in his homework.

FAVOURITE

What is your **favourite** toy? Which toy do you like best?
Bouncing Baby is a **favourite** with everyone in his family. They all love him very much.

FEAR

To **fear** something is to be afraid of something. Some people **fear** snakes.
Most cats **fear** large dogs.
Olly Owl does not **fear** the dark.

FEAST

A **feast** is a rich meal prepared for some special event. Chief Chef prepared a huge **feast** to celebrate Bouncing Baby's birthday. Everyone ate many good things at the party.

FEATHER

A **feather** is very light. Birds are covered with **feathers**. **Feathers** grow out from a bird's skin. Carol Canary has pretty, yellow **feathers**.

FEBRUARY

February is the second month of the year. It has 28 days except in leap years when it has 29 days.
If the last two figures of a year make a number which can be exactly divided by 4, then that year is a leap year.

FEEL

Feel Clarence Cat's fur. Touch it and **feel** how soft it is.
If you are happy you **feel** glad.
If you are unhappy you **feel** sad.

FEET

People and animals stand on their **feet**. People have two **feet**; most animals have four **feet**. We use our **feet** to walk and run and jump and skip.

FEMALE

Natalie Niece is a girl. She is a **female** child. When she grows up she will be a woman.
Camilla Cow is a **female** animal. She is the mother of Cassy Calf.

FENCE

There is a wire **fence** around Farmer Brown's farm. The animals cannot get outside the **fence**. The **fence** around Bobby Boy's garden is made of wood.

FERRY

A **ferry** is a boat that takes cars or people or goods across a stretch of water.

FESTIVAL

A **festival** is a time of special celebration. Many people enjoy the Christmas **festival**, celebrating the birth of Christ, and have a feast on Christmas Day.

FEVER

David was away from school because he was ill with a **fever**. He had a high temperature.

FEW

There are not many errors in Bobby Boy's homework, only a **few**.
There are **few** children who do not like sweets.

FIELD

A **field** is a piece of flattish land with few, or no, trees. A **field** may be used for growing crops or for pasture. Animals graze in grassy **fields**.

FIFTEEN

Fifteen is 5 more than 10. When you add 5 and 5 and 5 you have 15.

FIGHT

When people **fight** they argue and hit one another. Soldiers are trained to **fight** with weapons. A **fight** ends when one side surrenders.

FILL

Mother will **fill** Bouncing Baby's bottle with milk. The bottle will be full. It will hold no more milk.

FILM

A **film** is a moving picture. We can watch a **film** at the cinema or on television. Do you like to watch cartoon **films**?

FINAL

The **final** day of the year is December 31st. It is the last day of the year.
In the word '**final**', 'l' is the **final** letter. It comes last.

FIND

Bobby Boy will **find** the lost ball. He is looking for it and will see it.

FINE

A **fine** day is sunny and clear. Tommy Teacher is a **fine** teacher. He is a very good teacher.
Silkworms spin **fine**, soft thread.

FINGER

A **finger** is a part of the hand. Each hand has four **fingers** and one thumb. The **finger** next to the thumb is called the **forefinger** .

FINISH

Baby Brother will **finish** his dinner. He will eat all his dinner.

FIRE

When something is burning we have a **fire**. Beware! **Fire** is hot.
We use a **fire** to keep warm but sometimes a **fire** will burn down a house or a factory.

FIRE-FIGHTER

A **fire-fighter** is a person who is trained to put out fires. A **fire-fighter** belongs to a fire brigade. **Fire-fighters** race to a fire in a fire-engine.

FIREPLACE

A **fireplace** is a place built to hold a fire. A **fireplace** in a room is usually made of brick or stone and has a chimney leading up from it to take away the smoke.

FIRST

Albert Ape got to the party **first**. He arrived before anyone else.
'A' is the **first** letter of the English alphabet.
'A' comes before all the other letters.

FISH

A **fish** is a swimming animal with scales that lives in water.
A **fish** has gills with which to breathe. Some **fish** are good to eat. Sometimes Father and his friend go to the stream to **fish**.

FISHMONGER

A **fishmonger** is a person who sells all kinds of fish and sea-food. Bobby Boy buys fish for Clarence Cat from the **fishmonger**

FIST

A totally closed hand is called a **fist**. When people fight they sometimes hit each other with their **fists**.

FIT

Does Belinda Ballerina's new dress **fit** her? Is it the right size?
If a person is **fit** they are healthy.
We need exercise to keep **fit**.

FIVE

Five is a number. **Five** is one more than four.
If you add 3 and 2 you have **5**.

FIX

Baby Brother's toy truck is broken. Dad will **fix** it. He will mend it.

FLAG

A **flag** is a piece of cloth, usually with a pattern or design on it, which is used as the emblem or sign of a country or organisation.
Each country has its own **flag**.

FLAMINGO

A **flamingo** is a large wading bird which lives where the weather is warm. A **flamingo** has a long neck, very long legs and feathers which can vary from pink to bright red.

FLAVOUR

Filly Foal likes the **flavour** of peppermint. She likes the smell and the taste of peppermint. Bobby Boy bought fifteen sweets, each one of which had a different **flavour**.

FLOAT

A boat will **float** on water. It will stay on top of the water and not sink.
A balloon will **float** in the air.

FLOOD

A **flood** is a large amount of water covering what is usually dry land. Heavy rain may cause a river to burst its banks and **flood** the fields.

FLOOR

A **floor** is the bottom part of a room. Bouncing Baby crawls on the **floor**.

FLORIST

A **florist** is someone who grows or sells flowers.
Natalie Niece bought a bunch of flowers from the **florist**.

FLOWER

A **flower** is the blossom of a plant. **Flowers** produce seeds. There are many different kinds of **flowers**. Many **flowers** have a lovely smell and are pretty to look at.

FLY

A **fly** is a small insect with two wings. Flies carry germs which spread disease.
To **fly** is to move through the air. Birds flap their wings to **fly**. Arnold Aircraft has huge engines to make him **fly**.

FLYOVER

A **flyover** is a road built high above the ground to allow traffic to pass over another road below.

FOAL

A **foal** is a young horse, donkey or zebra.
Filly **Foal** is a young, female horse. When she grows up she will be a mare.

FOLD

We **fold** a letter to make it fit into an envelope. We bend the paper over on itself.

FOLLOW

Digger Dog likes to **follow** Bobby Boy. He likes to walk behind him. Night **follows** day. Night comes after day.

FOOD

All living things need **food** to stay alive. Animals, plants and people eat or drink **food** to live and grow.

FOOL

A **fool** is a person without sense. A **fool** often acts in a silly way.
Do not play the **fool** at school!

FOOT

A **foot** is the part of the body on which people and animals stand.
The **foot** of anything is the lowest part. Can you see a number at the **foot** of this page?

FOOTPATH

A **footpath** is too narrow for cars or other vehicles and is where people may only walk.
A winding **footpath** led through the forest.

FOREST

A **forest** is a large area of land which is covered with many trees. Dilly Deer lives in a **forest** with her friends.

FORGET

Did you **forget** to brush you teeth?
Did you fail to remember to brush them?
Mickey Monkey did not **forget** the party!

FORK

A **fork** is a piece of cutlery. We use a **fork** to pick up food from our plates. A **fork** has a long handle and two or more prongs for holding the food.

FORTY

Forty is a number.
If you add 20 and 20 you have **40**.
4 x 10 = **40**.

FOSSIL

A **fossil** is the hardened remains or impression of an animal or plant and is found in rock.
Bobby Boy found a **fossil** of a fern in a piece of coal.

FOUND

Bobby boy **found** his ball. If you **find** something that was lost, you have **found** it.

FOUR

Four is a number. **Four** is one more than three. 3 + 1 = **4**.
Filly Foal has **four** legs and **four** hooves.

FOURTEEN

Fourteen is a number. **Fourteen** is four more than ten.
If you add 7 and 7 you get **14**.

FOWL

A **fowl** is a bird. Henrietta Hen is a **fowl** and lays eggs for us to eat.

FOX

A **fox** is a wild animal which looks a little like a dog.
Freddy **Fox** has a red, furry coat and a bushy tail.

FREEZE

When the weather is very cold the pond will **freeze**. The water will turn to ice. It is very dangerous to try and walk on a **frozen** pond.

FRIDAY

Friday is the sixth day of the week. **Friday** is the day after Thursday and the day before Saturday.

FRIEND

Eric Elf is Daniel Dwarf's **friend**. He likes him very much. Bobby Boy has many **friends**. He invited all his **friends** to his birthday party.

FRIGHT

When something suddenly scares you it gives you a **fright**.

FROG

A **frog** is a small, wild, leaping creature which lives both on land and in the water. Frankie **Frog** has strong back legs and can jump a long way.

FRONT

The part of anything that faces forward is the **front**. Your nose is on the **front** of your face. Daffy Duck and Lucy Lamb sit in **front** seats when they visit the circus.

FRUIT

A **fruit** is the part of some plants that contains seeds. Apples and oranges are **fruit** but there are many other kinds. Eating **fruit** is good for your health.

FRY

Mother Goose will **fry** dozens of doughnuts for the party. She will cook them in hot fat or oil in a **frying** pan.

FUEL

This is any substance which can be burned to make a fire. Oil, coal and wood are **fuels**.

FULL

Colin Conductor rang the bell because Big Bus was **full**. There was no room for anyone else. Bouncing Baby's bottle is **full** and it can hold no more milk.

FUR

Fur is the soft coat of hair that covers the bodies of many animals. Bertie Bear has thick, brown **fur**. Reginald Rabbit has soft, white **fur**.

FURNISH

Mother Goose will **furnish** the party with doughnuts. She will provide enough doughnuts for everyone. Dad plans to **furnish** a bedroom for Baby Brother. He will put furniture of a smaller size into it.

FURNITURE

People have **furniture** in their homes. Chairs, tables, beds and wardrobes are **furniture**.

Gg

GAIN
Bouncing Baby will **gain** weight as he grows. His weight will increase.

GALAXY
A **galaxy** is a group of stars in the night sky.
The Milky Way **Galaxy** contains the solar system.

GALE
A **gale** is a very strong wind.
A **gale** blew the branch off the tree.

GALLOP
A **gallop** is a quick run. Filly Foal will **gallop** to the circus. She will run as fast as she can.

GAME
When we play a **game** we have fun. We play a **game** by rules.
Baseball is a **game** with a bat and a ball.
Bridge and whist are card **games**.

GARAGE
A **garage** is a building where motor-vehicles are stored or repaired.
Both Bully Bulldozer and Jontie Jeep are kept in a **garage**.

GARDEN
A **garden** is a piece of land, usually near a house, which is used for growing flowers and vegetables.
Digger Dog and the children play on the lawn in their **garden**.

GARLIC
This is an onion-like plant.
Garlic has a strong taste and smell and is used in cooking.
Do you like the taste of **garlic**?

GARMENT
A **garment** is any article of clothing.
Belinda Ballerina's favourite **garment** is her beautiful, red dress.

GAS
A **gas** is a substance like air.
There are many different **gases** and some burn. We use **gas** for cooking and heating.

GASP
People often **gasp** when they get a surprise or a fright. They take a sudden, short breath.
The members of the audience all **gasp** when they watch Batty Bat, the acrobat, perform on the tight-rope.

GATE
A **gate** is the part in a wall or a fence that opens to let us through.
A **gate** is like a door.
Digger Dog will escape from the garden if you forget to close the **gate**.

GATHER

Natalie Niece will **gather** some flowers. She will pick some flowers. Squeaky Squirrel will **gather** nuts in the autumn. He will collect the nuts together in one place as food for the winter.

GEM

A **gem** is a precious stone or jewel. Diamonds, rubies, emeralds and sapphires are **gems**.

GENTLE

Filly Foal is a **gentle**, little horse. She is quiet and tame. Digger Dog is a **gentle** dog. He is kind and friendly.

GEOGRAPHY

Geography is the study of the earth's surface together with its climates, countries, peoples, animals, plants, industries and products.

GERM

A **germ** is a tiny, living thing which can cause disease. **Germs** are too small to be seen except with a microscope.

GHOST

A **ghost** is the spirit of a dead person appearing to the living. The **ghost** of a brave knight haunted the castle.

GIANT

A **giant** is a person or thing that is big and strong. Geoffrey **Giant** is a huge man. There are **giant**, redwood trees in California.

GIFT

Daffy Duck gave Sammy Seal a **gift**. She gave him a present.

GIRAFFE

A **giraffe** is a very tall animal from Africa with a long neck and spotted skin. George **Giraffe** eats leaves from tall trees.

GIRL

Natalie Niece is a **girl**. She is a female child. When she grows up she will be a woman.

GIVE

Daffy Duck likes to **give** presents to her friends. If someone **gives** you something you do not have to pay for it.

GLAD

Digger Dog is **glad** that he found his bone. He is happy that he found the bone. Sammy Seal was **glad** to see all his friends at the party.

GLASS

This is a hard substance which it is easy to break. Light passes through **glass** so window-panes are made of **glass**.
We drink milk from a **glass**.

GLASSES

People who do not see well often wear **glasses** to improve their sight.
Eye **glasses** are made from a special kind of glass.
Dark **glasses** protect our eyes from the sun's rays.

GLIDER

Gilbert **Glider** is an aeroplane without an engine. He **glides** through the sky on currents of air.

GLOVES

We wear **gloves** on our hands to keep them warm and to protect them.
Gloves have separate places for each thumb and each finger.

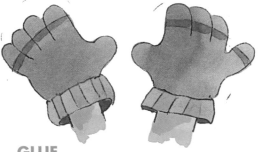

GLUE

This is a sticky substance used for sticking things together. Dad fixed the broken toy with **glue**.

GNAW

Digger Dog will **gnaw** his bone. He will bite and chew on his bone.

GO

This means to move from one place to another. When Bobby Boy and Natalie Niece **go** to school Bouncing Baby and Baby Brother **go** to the park.

GOAL

Bobby Boy kicked the ball between the **goal-posts** and scored the winning **goal**.

GOAT

A **goat** is a domestic animal. The male is called a 'Billy' and has horns and a beard. We get milk from the female or 'Nanny'. Gertie **Goat** is very active.

GOLD

This is a beautiful, precious, yellow metal.
Aunty Ivy has a **gold** ring on her finger. Dad has a watch made of **gold**.

GOLDFISH

Gilly **Goldfish** is a small gold-coloured fish. She lives in a glass bowl.

GOLF

Golf is an outdoor game, played on a special course, in which a small, solid ball is hit with sticks called clubs into a series of holes.

GOOD

Bouncing Baby is a **good** boy. He is well-behaved.
Mother Goose bakes very **good** cakes.
Her cakes are excellent.

GOODBYE

We say "**Goodbye**" to our friends when they go away.

GOOSE

A **goose** is a large bird that can swim. A **goose** looks a little like a duck but it has a longer neck. The meat of **geese** is good to eat.

GORILLA

A **gorilla** is a very large, man-like ape which lives in Africa. A **gorilla** is the largest kind of ape. Guy **Gorilla** is very strong.

GOVERNMENT

A **government** is a group of people who control, rule and administer the laws of a country.

GRAB

If you **grab** something you snatch hold of it quickly.
Digger Dog **grabbed** his bone and ran.

GRACE

We say **grace** at mealtimes. We say a short prayer of thanks for our food.

GRAIN

Grain is the seed of plants like wheat, barley and oats.
A **grain** is one of the very tiny pieces of which things like sugar are made up.

GRAMMAR

This is the science of language. We learn the rules for the correct use of words when we learn **grammar**.

GRAND

This means great, splendid or important.
Kings and queens often live in **grand** palaces.

GRANDCHILD

Someone's **grandchild** is the child of that person's daughter or son. You are the **grandchild** of your grandparents.

GRANDFATHER

Your father's father is your **grandfather**.
Your mother's father is also your **grandfather**.

GRANDMOTHER

Your mother's mother is your **grandmother**.
Your father's mother is your **grandmother** too.

GRAPE

A **grape** is a small, round fruit that grows in bunches on a vine.
A **grape** is red, purple or pale green.
Grapes can be made into wine.

GRAPEFRUIT

A **grapefruit** is a round, yellow, sour fruit, like an orange but larger.

GRASS

Grass is a plant with long, narrow, green leaves. **Grass** grows on a lawn or in fields. Some animals eat **grass**.

GRASSHOPPER

A **grasshopper** is an insect with strong, long legs for jumping.

GRATEFUL

If you are **grateful** you feel pleased and thankful.
Most people would be **grateful** for a hot meal on a cold day.

GRAVY

This is a liquid food. **Gravy** is made from the juices that come from meat during cooking.
We pour **gravy** over our meat and vegetables.

GRAZE

Camilla Cow and Dolly Donkey go to the field to **graze**. They feed on the growing grass.

GREAT

This means large or important.
Mount Everest is a **great** mountain.
The Olympic Games are a **great** sporting event.

GREEDY

Please do not be **greedy**.
If you are a **greedy** person you want more than your share.

GREEN

Green is a colour.
In summer the leaves of the trees are **green**.

GREET

Sammy Seal will **greet** his friends when they come to his party.
He will give them a warm welcome.

GREY

Grey is a colour.

... lly Elephant has **grey** skin.

... olly Donkey has a **grey**, furry ...oat.

GRILL

... When we **grill** food we place it on a ...etal frame to cook under the source ...f the heat.

GRIND

... **grind** means to crush into small ...ieces or into powder.

...he grocer will **grind** the coffee ...eans in a **grinder**.

GROCER

... **grocer** is a person who sells ...ood.

...other Goose went to the **grocer's** ...op to buy coffee, sugar and flour.

GROUND

The **ground** is the surface of the earth.

Farmer Brown plants seeds in the **ground**.

GROUP

A **group** is a number of people or things together.

A **group** of children built sand-castles on the beach.

GROWL

Dogs **growl**. When Digger Dog **growls** he makes a low, angry, rumbling sound in his throat.

GROWN

Bouncing Baby has **grown**. He has become larger.

Trigger Tree has **grown** taller.

GROWN-UP

When you have finished growing you will be a **grown-up**. You will be an adult.

GRUMPY

This means ill-tempered and rude.

No-one liked the **grumpy**, old woman who found fault with everyone and everything.

GRUNT

Pigs **grunt**.

When Piggles Pig **grunts** he makes a short, deep noise in his throat.

GUARANTEE

A **guarantee** is a promise to replace goods which become faulty within a set time.

If you **guarantee** to do something, you promise that you will do it.

GUARD

A **guard** watches against danger to people or property. A **life-guard** keeps us safe at the swimming pool or beach.

GUESS

Can you **guess** the number of sweets in the jar?
Can you think of the right number?

GUEST

A **guest** is a visitor at your home. There were many **guests** at Sammy Seal's party.

GUIDE

Baby Brother does not know the way to school. Bobby Boy will **guide** him. He will show him the way.

GUINEA-PIG

A **guinea-pig** is a small, fat animal, from South America. Ginger **Guinea-Pig** looks somewhat like a rat, with short ears and no tail.

GUITAR

A **guitar** is a musical instrument with six strings. You play a **guitar** with your fingers.

GUM

This is a sticky material. You can stick things together with **gum**. The firm flesh in which teeth grow is called a **gum**.

GUN

A **gun** is a weapon which kills. A **gun** has a metal barrel for firing bullets.

GUST

A sudden, strong rush of air is called a **gust**.
A **gust** of wind blew Dainty Doll's umbrella inside out.

GUY

A **guy** is a rope or chain to steady or hold something in position – as the ropes on a tent do.

GYMNASIUM

A **gymnasium** is a large room fitted out with special apparatus where people exercise to keep fit and healthy.

GYMNASTICS

Gymnastics are exercises for strengthening the body.
A **gymnast** is a person who is an expert in **gymnastics**.

Hh

HABIT

A **habit** is a thing that you do almost without thinking because you have done it so often.
Brushing your teeth is a good **habit**.

HAD

This bottle **had** milk in it but it does not have any in it now.
Baby Brother **had** a kite but it flew away. He owned a kite but he does not have it now.

HADDOCK

A **haddock** is a sea-fish that is good to eat. A **haddock** is like a cod but smaller.

HAIR

Hair grows on the heads and bodies of animals and people.
Hair is like fine threads.
Hair on most animals is called fur.

HALF

A **half** is one of the two equal parts of anything.
Mother cut the cake in **half**.
A **half** of 10 is 5.

HALL

A **hall** is the part of a house which is just inside the front door.
A very big room where meetings are held is called a **hall**.

HAM

Ham is meat.
We get **ham** from the upper part of a pig's hind leg.

HAMBURGER

A **hamburger** is a round, fried cake of minced beef that we usually eat in a bread bun.

HAND

A **hand** is the end part of an arm which can pick up things and hold them.

HANDLE

We hold things by the **handle**.
Cups, cutlery, doors, hammers, pails and suitcases all have **handles**.
If you **handle** something you touch it with your hand.

HANDSOME

Handsome means good-looking.
We usually say that men and boys are **handsome**.

HANG

When we **hang** something we fasten it at the top and let it swing freely at the bottom.
We **hang** our clothes in a wardrobe.
Dad will **hang** his hat on a hook.

HAPPEN

The boy saw an accident **happen**.
He saw an accident take place.
He just **happened** to see it.
He saw the accident by chance.

HAPPY

If you are **happy** you feel very
pleased and full of joy.
The new dress made Belinda
Ballerina **happy**.

HARBOUR

A **harbour** is a sheltered place
where ships can stay safely when
they are not at sea.

HARD

Rock, glass and steel are **hard**.
They are not soft.
Hard sums are not easy to do.

HARP

A **harp** is a large musical
instrument with strings that are
stretched across its frame and
played with the fingers.

HARVEST

Harvest is the time or season when
the ripe crops are gathered in.
To **harvest** is to reap and collect
the crops which are ready.

HAS

Dainty Doll **has** an umbrella.
She owns an umbrella.
The jar **has** sweets in it.
The jar contains sweets.

HAT

A **hat** is worn on the head to keep it
warm or to protect it.
Bouncing Baby wears a
woollen **hat**.
A fireman wears a hard **hat**.

HATCH

To **hatch** means to break out of an
egg to be born. Birds, fish, snakes
and insects **hatch**.
A ship's **hatch** is the opening in the
deck through which the cargo is
loaded.

HAVE

To **have** means to hold or to own or
to experience.
I **have** a ball in my hand.
I **have** a gold ring.
I **have** a good time at parties.

HAWK

A **hawk** is a bird with a hooked
beak and strong, curved claws.
A **hawk** hunts and eats small birds
and animals.

HAY

Hay is dried grass that is used to
feed horses and cattle.

HE

Piggles Pig is fat because **he** eats a lot.

David had a fever but **he** is better today.

He is the male person or animal spoken about.

HEAD

The **head** is the top part of an animal's or person's body that contains the brain.

Chief Chef is the **head** chef.

He is the person in charge.

HEALTH

Bobby Boy is in good **health**; he is fit and well.

David is in poor **health**; he is ill with a fever.

HEAR

You **hear** sounds with your ears.

Did you **hear** the music?

Did you listen to it?

HEART

The **heart** is the part of the body that pumps blood round the body.

The **heart** of a thing is the centre or main part of it.

HEAT

Heat is the feeling of warmth that comes from the sun or a fire or a radiator.

When we **heat** something we make it warm or hot.

HEAVY

Things that weigh a lot are **heavy**.

Heavy things are hard to lift.

Elly Elephant is very **heavy**.

HEIGHT

Height is how tall someone is or how high something is.

We measure **height** from the ground upwards.

HELP

To **help** is to make things easier for someone else by doing something useful.

Gracie Gosling will **help** Mother Goose bake the cakes.

HEMISPHERE

Half of a sphere or half of the Earth's surface is called a **hemisphere**.

Our Earth can be divided into Eastern or Western **Hemispheres**, or into Northern and Southern **Hemispheres**.

HEN

A **hen** is a female bird.

A **hen** lays eggs.

When the eggs hatch the **hen** takes care of the chicks.

HER

Her means belonging to a girl, a woman or a female animal.

Dainty Doll has lost **her** umbrella.

Filly Foal will let you stroke **her** head.

HERD

A **herd** is a number of animals together.
Farmer Brown has a large **herd** of cows and a small **herd** of goats.

HERE

Here is the place where you are at this time.

HID

Digger Dog **hid** his bone in a hole in the ground.
He put his bone out of sight.

HIGH

The kite flew **high** into the air. It flew a long way above the ground.
A mountain is **high**. It is a long way from the bottom to the top.

HILL

A **hill** is a piece of ground that is higher than the ground around it but not as high as a mountain.

HIT

To **hit** is to knock or strike a thing or a person.
Dad **hit** the nail with a hammer.
When people fight they **hit** each other with their fists.

HIVE

A **hive** is a small house in which bees are kept.
A **hive** of bees is a large number of bees living together.

HOLD

To **hold** is to have something in your hands.
A **hold** is the place inside a ship or an aircraft where the cargo is kept.

HOLE

A **hole** is a hollow place, or an opening, or a gap made in something.
There is a **hole** in the fence.
Bobby Boy has a **hole** in his shoe.
Reginald Rabbit lives in a **hole** in the ground.

HOLIDAY

A **holiday** is a day, or days, of rest from school or work.
Christmas is a **holiday** for many people.

HOLLOW

If a thing is **hollow** it has an empty space inside it. It is not solid.
Many rubber balls are **hollow**.
A **hollow** is also a kind of hole.

HOME

The place where you live is your **home**.
A hive is Buzzy Bee's **home**.
A cave is Batty Bat's **home**.

HOMEWORK

Homework is the work that you bring from school to do at home.

HONEST

Bobby Boy is an **honest** boy. He never cheats or steals or tells lies. Everyone likes him because he can be trusted.

HONEY

Honey is the sweet, sticky food that bees make from the drops of nectar they collect from flowers.

HOOF

A **hoof** is the hard part of a foot of some animals such as the horse, cow, sheep and pig.
We call the whole of a foot of such animals a **hoof**.

HOOK

A **hook** is a piece of bent metal for catching hold of something or for hanging things on.
You hang your coat on a **hook**.
An angler has a **hook** to catch fish.

HOP

To **hop** is to leap on one foot or to move in jumps like a frog, a bird or a kangaroo.
Kathy Kangaroo can **hop** very far.

HORSE

A **horse** is a strong animal that is used for riding or for pulling carts and carriages.

HORSESHOE

A **horseshoe** is a U-shaped, flat piece of metal nailed to the underside of a horse's hoof to protect it.

HOSPITAL

A **hospital** is a place where people who are ill or hurt are cared for. Nice Nurse works in a **hospital**.

HOT

Fire is **hot**. If a thing is **hot** it is very, very warm. Never touch **hot** things because they will burn you.

HOTEL

A **hotel** is a building where people pay to have meals and a room in which to sleep when they are away from home.

HOUR

An **hour** is a measure of time. One **hour** is sixty minutes.
There are twenty-four **hours** in a day.

HOUSE

A **house** is a building in which people live.

HOW

How is a word which means 'In what way?' or 'To what extent?' or 'In what condition?'

How did the accident happen?

How tall is George Giraffe?

Doc Doctor said, "**How** do you feel today?"

HUG

Mother gave Bouncing Baby a **hug**. She put her arms around him and held him close with a gentle squeeze.

HUGE

Elly Elephant is **huge**. She is very, very big.

Ronnie Rhinoceros is **huge** too. He is very large like Elly.

HUNGRY

When your stomach feels empty you become **hungry**.

If you are **hungry** you either need or want something to eat.

HURRY

When we **hurry** we move quickly. Albert Ape was in a **hurry** to get to the party, so he ran very fast.

HURT

Baby Brother cried with pain when he fell and **hurt** his knee.

To **hurt** is to cause pain or injury to a person or an animal.

HUSBAND

A **husband** is a man who is married.

HUSH

Hush! Keep quiet, Bouncing Baby is fast asleep. **Hush**! Stop making a noise or you will wake him.

HUT

A **hut** is a roughly-made, little hous or cabin.

The children built a **hut** in one corner of the garden.

HUTCH

A **hutch** is a little, wooden house o box in which a pet rabbit can be kept.

HYACINTH

A **hyacinth** is a sweet-smelling flower that grows from a bulb.

I

When you are speaking of yourself you use '**I**'.

Bobby Boy said, "**I** like Digger Dog and he likes me."

ICE

Ice is frozen water. It is hard and cold.

Beware! It is dangerous to skate on thin **ice**.

ICE-CREAM

Ice-cream is a frozen food that is made from cream, sugar and flavourings. Baby Brother likes chocolate **ice-cream**.

ICICLE

An **icicle** is a pointed, hanging spike of ice. **Icicles** form when dripping water freezes.

IDEA

An **idea** is a thought or plan you have in your mind.

Dad had an **idea** for an exciting holiday but he had no **idea** that it would cost so much.

IDENTICAL

When two or more things are the same in every detail, they are **identical**.

Identical twins are exactly alike.

IDENTIFY

To **identify** means to recognise or pick out a certain person or thing. Aunty Ivy can **identify** a hyacinth by its smell.

IDLE

Lazy Jack Jaguar is **idle**. He is not doing anything.

IF

You may go **if** it is fine.
You may go provided that it is fine.
If it rains I could take an umbrella.
Supposing that it rains I could take an umbrella.

IGLOO

An **igloo** is an Eskimo house that is shaped like a dome and made of blocks of hard snow.

IGNORANT

Uncle Harry is **ignorant** about sailing.

He knows nothing about sailing.

ILL

David is **ill**.
He has a fever.
He is not well.

ILLUSTRATE

Bobby Boy has written a story.
Now he will **illustrate** it.
He will draw pictures about the story.

IMAGINE

To **imagine** is to create a picture or an idea in your mind.
Baby Brother likes to **imagine** he is an engine driver.

IMPOLITE

Anyone showing bad manners and rudeness to others is **impolite**.
It is **impolite** to be greedy.

IMPORTANT

If something is **important** it is noteworthy.
Mount Everest is an **important** mountain.
Your birthday is an **important** day.

IN

Bertie Bear lives **in** a cave **in** the winter.
Please come **in**; the others will be here **in** a minute.
Digger Dog dug a hole **in** the garden.

INCH

An **inch** is a measure of length.
One **inch** equals 2.4 centimetres.

INCREASE

To **increase** is to make or become bigger.
If Piggles Pig eats much more he will **increase** in size.

INDEED

Belinda Ballerina is **indeed** happy with her new dress.
She is really happy.
George Giraffe is tall; **indeed** he is very tall.
George Giraffe is tall; in fact he is very tall.

INDOORS

You are **indoors** when you are inside a house or another building.
If it rains, Clarence Cat will stay **indoors**.

INFLAMMABLE

When something is **inflammable** it is easily set on fire.
Petrol and matches are **inflammable**.

INFLATE

To **inflate** is to blow or puff air or gas into something to make it swell out.
We **inflate** balloons.

INFORM

Mother will **inform** Tommy Teacher of David's illness.
She will tell him, "David is ill."

INK

Ink is a coloured liquid.
When we write with a pen we use ink.
Ink is used in the printing of books, newspapers and comics.

INSECT

An insect is a tiny animal with six legs.
Flies, ants, butterflies, gnats, bees and beetles are all insects.

INSIDE

Bouncing Baby is inside the house.
He is not outside, he is within.
Your brain is inside your head.

INTELLIGENT

Intelligent means able to learn and understand things quickly.

INTERESTED

To be interested means that you want to know or do something.

Bobby Boy is interested in reading and collecting autographs.

INTO

Jontie Jeep will go into the garage.
He will go inside the garage.
The wicked witch turned the prince into a frog.

INVENT

To invent is to design or make or think of something entirely new.
People who invent things often become famous.

INVITE

To invite is to ask someone politely to do something or to come to some place.
Albert Ape likes parties; will you invite him?

IRON

Iron is a hard, strong metal.
Horseshoes are made out of iron.
An iron is a machine that we heat and use to press the creases out of our clothes.

ISLAND

An island is a piece of land with water all round it.

ITCH

An itch is the prickly, tickling feeling in your skin that makes you want to scratch yourself.
Gnat bites itch.

IVY

Ivy is a climbing, evergreen plant with shiny, dark-green leaves.
Ivy clings to walls and trees by very small roots.

JACKET

A **jacket** is a short coat.
Farmer Brown wears a **jacket** with large checks.

JAGUAR

A **jaguar** is an animal much like a leopard but larger.
Jack **Jaguar** eats meat and fish. He is a good climber and an excellent swimmer as well.

JAIL

A **jail** is a prison. People who do bad things are sometimes put into **jail**.
A **jail** is a building with bars on the doors and windows.

JAM

Jam is a food made by boiling fruit and sugar together.
Many things crowded together so it is hard to move is called a **jam**.
Big Bus was delayed by a traffic **jam**.

JANUARY

January is the first month of the year.
It has thirty-one days.

JEEP

A **jeep** is a strong, four-wheel drive vehicle.
Jontie **Jeep** can travel safely across hilly country or very rough roads.

JELLY

Jelly is a clear, wobbly food made from fruit juice and sugar.
The children ate orange **jelly** and ice-cream at the party.

JEWEL

A **jewel** is a very valuable and beautiful stone, such as a diamond or a ruby.
Aunty Ivy wears a necklace made of **jewels** and gold.

JOG

To **jog** is to run at a slow, even pace or to shake or push against something with a jerk.
Some people go **jogging** to keep fit.
Please do not **jog** my elbow.

JOIN

To **join** is to fasten things together or to become a member of a group.
We all **join** hands to form a circle.
Batty Bat would like to **join** the circus.

JOINT

A **joint** is the place at which two things are joined together. The elbow is the **joint** between the wrist and the shoulder.

JOKE

A **joke** is something said or done to make people laugh.

JOLLY

Brian Baker is very **jolly**.
He is happy and full of fun.

JOURNEY

A **journey** is a trip.
To **journey** is to travel.
Arnold Aircraft will make a long
journey round the world.

JOY

Joy is a feeling of great happiness.
Bobby Boy jumped for **joy** when he
scored a goal.

JUDGE

The **judge** in a court of law sends
people to jail, or makes them pay a
fine for doing wrong.
A **judge** can also be a person
chosen to settle a quarrel or to
decide the winner in a contest.

JUG

A **jug** is a container with a handle
and a spout that is used for pouring
liquids.

JUICE

Juice is the liquid in fruit, meat and
vegetables.
Orange **juice** is sweet.
Lemon **juice** is sour.
We make gravy with meat **juice**.

JULY

July is the seventh month of the
year.
July has thirty-one days.

JUMP

To **jump** is to leap or spring into the
air. Kathy Kangaroo can **jump**
very far.
Filly Foal is too young to **jump** over
the high fence.

JUNE

June is the sixth month of the year.
June has thirty days.

JUNGLE

A **jungle** is a dense, over-grown
forest in a very hot country.
Jack Jaguar lives in a **jungle** in
South America.

JURY

A **jury** is a group of people in a
court of law who decide whether a
prisoner is guilty or not.
A **jury** can also be a group of
people chosen to decide winners in
a contest.

JUST

Just means fair and proper.
A judge must give a **just**
punishment.
Just means only.
Baby Brother is **just** a small boy.
Just means exactly.
This present is **just** what I wanted.

Kk

KALEIDOSCOPE

A **kaleidoscope** is a toy made from a tube, containing mirrors, in which bits of coloured glass make continually-changing, symmetrical patterns as the end of the tube is turned.

KANGAROO

A **kangaroo** is an Australian animal with strong hind legs for jumping.
A female **kangaroo** has a pouch in front in which she carries her baby.

KAYAK

A **kayak** is an Eskimo canoe made from animal skins stretched over a frame of bones or wood with an opening in the middle for the person to sit in and paddle.

KEEP

If you **keep** something you hold on to it as your own for a long time or forever.
Keep also means to have and take care of.
Farmer Brown **keeps** chickens.

KENNEL

Digger Dog sleeps in a **kennel** in the garden. Digger's little house is cosy and warm.

KERB

The **kerb** is the edge of the pavement or sidewalk next to the road.
It is dangerous to walk too close to the **kerb**.

KETCHUP

Ketchup is a tasty sauce made from tomatoes, mushrooms, sugar, vinegar, salt and spices.
Bobby Boy puts **ketchup** on his hamburger.

KETTLE

We boil water in a **kettle**.
A **kettle** is a pot with a lid, a handle and a spout.

KEY

A **key** is a piece of metal shaped to fit into a lock and used for locking and unlocking.
A **key** is also one of the parts on a typewriter, piano or computer that you press to make it work.

KEYBOARD

A **keyboard** is the set of keys on a piano, typewriter or computer.

KEYHOLE

A **keyhole** is a small opening in a lock into which a key is put to turn the lock.

KICK

When you **kick** something you hit it with your foot.
Bobby Boy will try to **kick** the football into the goal.
Hobby Horse does not **kick**.

KID

A **kid** is a young goat.
Aunty Ivy has a pair of **kid** gloves.
They are made of soft leather.

KILL

To **kill** means to make someone or something die.
Cats **kill** mice.

KILOGRAM

A **kilogram** is a measurement of weight equal to 1,000 grammes or 2.2046 pounds.
How much do you weigh?

KILOMETRE

A **kilometre** is a measurement of distance equal to 1,000 metres or 3280.8 feet.
How far can you swim?

KIMONO

A **kimono** is a long, loose, Japanese robe with wide sleeves.
It is fastened with a sash.

KIND

To be **kind** is to be gentle, friendly and helpful towards others.
A **kind** means a type or sort of a thing.
Which **kind** of ice-cream do you like best?

KING

Some countries have a **king**.
The **king** is the man who rules the country and its people.
A **king** wears a crown on a special occasion.

KIOSK

A **kiosk** is a small, covered stall that sells newspapers, magazines and sweets.
A small building for a public telephone is also called a **kiosk**.

KISS

To **kiss** is to touch people with your lips.
We usually **kiss** the people we love.

KITCHEN

A **kitchen** is a room where food is prepared and cooked.
Chief Chef works in a **kitchen**.

KITE

A **kite** is a toy made of paper or cloth on a light, wooden frame that flies in the wind at the end of a long string.

KITTEN

A **kitten** is a young cat.
When Clarence Cat was a **kitten** he liked to play with Mother's knitting wool.

KIWI

The **kiwi**, a bird of New Zealand, is both tailless and flightless and feeds only at night.

A **kiwi** fruit is a Chinese gooseberry.

KNEE

Your **knee** is the joint in the middle of your leg where it bends.

KNEEL

When you **kneel** you get down on your knees.

Some people **kneel** to pray.

KNIFE

A **knife** is a cutting tool with a sharp blade and a handle.

KNIGHT

In days of old a **knight** was a man in armour who fought on horseback for his king.

KNIT

Natalie Niece will **knit** a scarf. She will use long needles to weave loops of wool into material.

KNOB

A **knob** is a round lump at the end of or on the surface of a thing.

A round handle on a drawer or a door is called a **knob**.

KNOCK

To **knock** is to hit something either by accident or on purpose.

Please do not **knock** the dish off the table.

Albert Ape will **knock** on the door when he arrives at the party.

KNOT

When you fasten your shoelaces you make a **knot**.

The **knot** is the twisted part where the laces are tied together.

KNOW

To **know** is to recognise, or to understand, or to be sure about something.

We **know** our friends. We **know** that 3+3 makes 6. We **know** that water is wet.

KNOWLEDGE

Knowledge is all the information and facts that are known or can be learned.

Your **knowledge** is all the things that you know now.

KOALA

Katy **Koala** is a grey, furry, Australian animal like a small bear. She carries her babies in a pouch and feeds only on the leaves of the eucalyptus trees in which she lives.

LABEL

A **label** is a piece of paper or cardboard fastened to a thing telling what or whose it is, or where it is going.

LABORATORY

A **laboratory** is a room or building where scientific work and research are carried out.

LACE

Lace is a fine material with a pretty pattern of holes in it.
Dainty Doll's dress has been trimmed with **lace**.

A **lace** is the thin cord or leather thong used to fasten a boot or shoe.

LADDER

A **ladder** is a set of steps that we use to climb things. It is made of two long pieces of wood, metal or rope joined by rungs.

LADY

A **lady** is a kind and polite woman.
Aunty Ivy is a **lady**.

LADYBIRD

A **ladybird** is a small, red or yellow, flying insect with black spots.

LAMB

A **lamb** is a baby sheep.
Lucy **Lamb** likes to run and jump and skip about.

LAME

Poor Ossie Ostrich is **lame**. He is not able to walk properly because his foot is hurt.

LAMP

A **lamp** gives light when and where we want it.
Street **lamps** come on at dusk.
A lighthouse has a powerful **lamp** that shines across the sea at night.

LAND

Land is the solid part of the Earth's surface that is not covered by water.
To **land** is to come down from the air on to the ground or water.

LANGUAGE

Language is words and sounds used by people when they write and speak.
There are thousands of **languages** but English is the most-used **language**.

LAP

When Mother is sitting down she holds Bouncing Baby on her **lap**.
Once round a race track is a **lap**.

LARDER

A **larder** is a small room or a cupboard where food is kept.

LARGE

Elly Elephant is not little; she is **large**.
Geoffrey Giant is a very **large** man.

LAST

Last means after all the others.
Snowy Snail came **last** in the race.
Last also means to go on for some time.
How long did the circus **last**?

LATE

The party begins at four o'clock so, please be on time, don't be **late**.

LAUGH

People **laugh** when they see something funny or hear a good joke.
The circus clowns made Bobby Boy **laugh** out loud.

LAUNDRY

Laundry is clothing that needs to be washed.
A **laundry** is a place where clothes are washed and ironed.

LAW

A **law** is a rule or set of rules made by the government that everyone in the country should obey.

LAWN

A **lawn** is a stretch of grass, usually in a garden, that is kept closely cut.

LAY

Lay means to place or put something down.
Lay your book on the table.
Lay also means to produce an egg.
Birds **lay** eggs.

LAZY

Albert Ape is **lazy**. He does not want to do any work.

LEAD

To **lead** is to go first and show others where to go or what to do.
The strap that fits on to a dog's coll is called a **lead**.

LEAF

A **leaf** is one of the thin, flat, gree parts that grow on trees and other plants.

LEAK

A **leak** is a hole or a crack through which liquid or gas passes in or out. A **leak** in a boat lets water get in. Gas can escape through a **leak** in a pipe.

LEAN

To **lean** is to bend over from an upright position toward something. Do you **lean** on your desk at school? Dad will **lean** the ladder against the wall.

LEAP

A **leap** is a big jump. To **leap** is to spring or jump into the air. Frankie Frog can **leap** very far.

LEARN

To **learn** is to find out about things or to get to know how to do something.
When did you **learn** to read?

LEATHER

Leather is a material made from animal skins. **Leather** is used to make shoes, bags, gloves and many other things.

LEAVE

Please **leave** the book on the table when you **leave**.
Please let the book stay on the table when you go away.

LEFT

Left is on the side opposite to right. Face north and **left** is on the side that is towards the west.
Bobby Boy writes with his **left** hand.

LEG

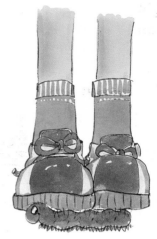

A **leg** is a part of the body.
We stand, walk and run using our **legs**.
A person has two **legs**.
Filly foal has four **legs**.
A centipede has many **legs**.

LEMON

A **lemon** is a sour, pale yellow fruit. We make **lemonade** from **lemon** juice, sugar and water.

LEND

To **lend** is to let another have or use for a short time something of yours which they will return.
Will you **lend** me your ladder for today?

LENGTH

Length is how long something is. Measure the distance from one end to the other to find the **length**.

LEOPARD

A **leopard** is a large, wild animal of the cat family that is found in Africa and Asia.
Leonard **Leopard** has dull yellow fur spotted with black.

LESSON

A **lesson** is something that has been or is to be learned.
The time when we are being taught is called a **lesson**.

LETTER

A **letter** is a sign used for writing words. A, B and C are **letters**.
A **letter** is a written message that is put in an envelope and sent to someone.

LETTUCE

A **lettuce** is a vegetable that can be eaten raw in salads.
Letty **Lettuce** has large, crisp, green leaves.

LEVEL

Level means flat and even.
An ice-rink is **level**.

LIBRARY

A **library** is a room or a building where collections of books are kept.
Public **Libraries** lend books.

LICK

If you **lick** something you move your tongue over it.
We **lick** lollipops.

LIFE

Life is the time between birth and death.
Life is being alive. People, animals and plants have **life**.

LIFEBOAT

A **lifeboat** is a strong boat built for going out to sea in bad weather to save people from drowning.

LIGHT

Light is a brightness by which we are able to see things.
We get **light** from the sun and from lamps.
Light also means not heavy. Feathers are **light**.

LIGHTHOUSE

A **lighthouse** is a tower topped with a bright light that shines out over the sea at night to warn sailors of danger.

LIKE

If you **like** someone or something you are fond of them.
Do you **like** lollipops?
Like can also mean the same or almost the same as another person or thing.
A wolf is **like** a dog.

LILAC

Lilac is a bush with white or pale purple blossoms that smell very sweet.
The colour **lilac** is pale pink or purple.

LIMB

An arm, a leg or a wing is a **limb**.
A branch of a tree is called a **limb**.

LIMIT

A **limit** is a boundary or point at which something ends or must end.
Keep within the speed **limit** until you have passed the city **limit**.

LIMP

To **limp** is to step or walk lamely because you have hurt your leg or foot.

LINE

A **line** is a long, narrow mark. You can draw a straight **line** or a wavy **line**.
If you stand in **line** you stand in a row.

LION

A **lion** is a strong, wild animal of the cat family.
Leo **Lion** has brownish-yellow skin and a mane that grows round his face.

LIQUID

A **liquid** can be poured. A **liquid** is wet and flows freely, like water, milk or oil.

LISTEN

When we **listen** we pay attention and make an effort to hear something.
Do you like to **listen** to music?

LITTER

Litter is bits of paper or rubbish left lying about.
A number of young animals born to the same mother at the same time is called a **litter**.

LITTLE

Little means small.
Baby Brother is a **little** boy.

LIVE

(pronounced as in 'hive')
Beware! This wire is **live**.
It carries electric current.

LIVE

(pronounced as in 'give')
Some trees **live** for a hundred years or more.
Where is your home? Where do you **live**?

LOAD

A **load** is something carried.
The cart carried a **load** of hay.
To **load** is to put things on or into something that is used for carrying.

LOAF

A **loaf** is bread baked as one piece into some special shape.

LOCK

A **lock** is a fastening for a door, a gate, a drawer or a box that is opened with its own special key.

LOG

A **log** is a piece of wood cut from the branches or the trunk of a tree. The daily record of the journey of a ship or an aircraft is called a **log**.

LOLLIPOP

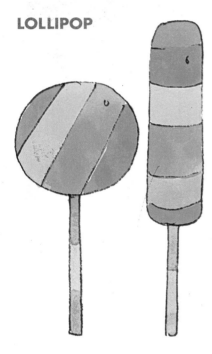

A **lollipop** is a big, hard sweet on the end of a stick.

LONG

This means measuring a lot in length or time. The moon is a **long** way from Earth. A year is a **long** time.

LOOK

To **look** is to turn your eyes in order to see something.
Stop, **look** and listen before you cross the road.

LOST

If something is **lost** you no longer have it.
Bobby Boy **lost** his ball.

LOUD

A **loud** noise is very easy to hear. Caw-Caw Crow has a **loud** voice.

LOVE

If you **love** someone or something you like them or it very, very much.
Mother Goose **loves** Gracie Gosling.
Albert Ape **loves** parties!

LOW

Low means not high or tall.
Filly Foal can jump a **low** fence. When Batty Bat is flying **low** he is near the ground.

LUCK

Luck is that which seems to happen or come to us by chance.
Luck can be good or it can be bad.

LULLABY

A **lullaby** is a gentle song that is sung to make a baby fall asleep. Bouncing Baby likes to listen to a **lullaby**.

LUNCH

Lunch is a meal that we eat in the middle of the day.

Mm

MACARONI

Macaroni is thin tubes of wheat-flour paste that we cook and eat.

MACHINE

A machine is a thing with several moving parts that work together to do some particular job.
Machines make work easier.
A lawn-mower is a machine for cutting grass.

MAGAZINE

A magazine is a thin book coming out each week or month with different stories and pictures in it.

MAGNIFY

To magnify something is to make it appear larger than it really is.
People use telescopes to magnify the stars.

MAIL

Mail is letters, cards or parcels sent by post.
The postman brings us mail.
If you mail a letter you put it in the mail-box .

MAIN

Main means the most important.
Dinner is the main meal of the day.

MAKE

To make is to create, build or produce something by putting different materials together.
Most birds make nests.
Make also means to cause to happen or to amount to.
Do not make a noise.
Two and two make four.
2+2 = 4.

MAN

A man is a fully-grown, male, human being.
When Bobby Boy grows up he will be a man like his father and Tommy Teacher.

MANAGE

To manage is to succeed in doing something even if it is difficult.
Will Elly Elephant manage to dance on her toes?
Manage also means to have charge or control of something.
Dad will manage the soccer team this year.

MANE

A mane is the long hair on the neck of a horse, lion, donkey or zebra.
Hobby Horse has a tangled mane.

MANNERS

Manners means our behaviour towards others.
A person with good manners is polite.

MANY

Many is a large number of persons or things.
There are many people in a crowd.
There are many trees in a forest.

MAP

A **map** is a flat drawing that shows details of the Earth's surface or some part of it.
Maps help us to find our way.

MARCH

March is the third month of the year.
March has thirty-one days.

MARGARINE

Margarine is a food which looks like butter, although it is made from vegetable oils and animal fats.

MARK

A **mark** is a stain or spot such as dirty **marks** on a clean floor.
A **mark** is the sign that shows what or where a thing is.
A **mark** on a piece of schoolwork is a letter or number to show how well you have done.

MARKET

A **market** is a place, with stalls, where people meet to buy and sell things.

MARMALADE

Marmalade is a kind of jam made from oranges, lemons, grapefruit or limes.

MARRY

When a man and a woman **marry**, they become husband and wife.

MASK

A **mask** is a covering to hide or to protect your face.
The children wore **masks** at the fancy dress party.

MASTER

A **master** is an owner, an expert or a person in charge.
Bobby Boy owns Digger Dog so he is his **master**.
Chief Chef is a **master** chef.
Captain Custard is the **master** of his ship.

MAT

A **mat** is a small rug used as a floor covering or as a foot-wiper, or it can be a small piece of thick material put on a table under a hot dish.

MATERIAL

Material is any stuff that is used in making something.
Cloth is the **material** for clothes.
Metal is the **material** for tools.
Wood is the **material** for tables and chairs.

MATHEMATICS

Mathematics is the study of numbers and measurement.
Arithmetic, algebra and geometry are part of **mathematics**.

MATTER

A **matter** is a thing or job that needs to be thought about or done. Road Safety is an important **matter**.

We say "What is the **matter**?" to find out what is wrong.

MAY

May is the fifth month of the year. **May** has thirty-one days.

MAYBE

Maybe means perhaps or possibly. **Maybe** Bobby Boy will find his ball today.

MAYOR

A **mayor** is the head of a town or city government.

Mr **Mayor** was chosen as the leader by the people who live in the town.

MEAL

A **meal** is the food eaten at any one time.

Breakfast, lunch, dinner, tea and supper are **meals**.

MEAN

If you **mean** to do something you intend to do it.

Bobby Boy and Baby Brother **mean** to learn to swim.

A person who is **mean** behaves in an unkind and selfish way.

MEASURE

We **measure** things to find out their size or weight or quantity.

We can **measure** the length, width, height, weight, depth or volume of a thing.

MEAT

Meat is the flesh of animals used as food.

Beef is **meat** from an ox, bull or cow.

Pork is **meat** from a pig.

MEDICINE

A doctor gives us **medicine** when we are ill.

Medicine is any liquid or pills that we must swallow in order to get well again.

MEET

To **meet** means to come together or join.

Batty Bat asked Albert Ape to **meet** him at the circus.

MELON

A **melon** is a large, many-seeded fruit with a green or yellow skin.

A **melon** grows on a vine.

MELT

To **melt** means to change from a solid to a liquid.

When the ice on a pond **melts**, it is turned into water by the sun's heat.

MEMORY

Memory is the ability to remember.
Bobby Boy does not forget things
because his **memory** is good.
Anything that we remember is called
a **memory**.

MEND

To **mend** is to repair a damaged
thing to make it useful again.
Dad will **mend** the broken toy.

MERRY

Merry means joyful and happy and
full of fun.
Did you have a **Merry** Christmas?

MESSAGE

When you send a **message**, you
send either spoken or written
information to someone elsewhere.

MIAOW

A **miaow** is the sound made by a
cat or kitten.
Clarence Cat cries, "**Miaow**!"
when he is hungry.

MICROWAVE

A **microwave** is a special kind of
oven. Food can be cooked very
quickly in Muriel **Microwave**.

MIDDLE

The **middle** is the centre or the part
of something that is at an equal
distance from each end or side.
Noon is the **middle** of the day.
The bull's-eye is the **middle** of the
target.

MIDNIGHT

Midnight is twelve o'clock at
night.
Midnight is the middle of the night.

MILE

A **mile** is a measurement of length.
A **mile** is the distance which is
equal to 5,280 feet, 1,760 yards or
1.6092 kilometres.

MILK

Milk is a white, liquid food that we
drink and use in cooking.
We get **milk** from cows and goats.
Farmer Brown has to **milk** his cows
twice a day.

MIND

Your **mind** is the part of you that
knows, thinks, has feelings and
decides your actions.
To **mind** is to take care of.
Mind also means to dislike or object
to something. Do you **mind** wet
weather? Daffy Duck does not
mind it at all.

MINI-BUS

A **mini-bus** is a small bus.
Minnie **Mini-Bus** has fewer seats
than Big Bus.

MINUTE

A **minute** is a short length of time equal to sixty seconds.
Sixty **minutes** of time equal one hour.

MIRROR

A **mirror** is a piece of glass, the back of which has a special coating enabling us to see our reflections.

MISCHIEF

Mischief is silly or annoying behaviour that causes trouble or harm to others.

MISS

To **miss** is to be unsuccessful in doing something or to feel sad about the absence of someone or something.
Hurry, Snowy Snail, or you will **miss** the party and your friends will **miss** you!

MIST

Mist is a thin fog or a very fine rain through which it is difficult to see.

MISTAKE

A **mistake** is an error or a fault. Tommy Teacher found one **mistake** in Bobby Boy's homework.

MIX

Mix means to mingle or to stir together.
Mother Goose will **mix** butter, sugar, flour, eggs and milk to make a cake.
Bobby Boy and Baby Brother **mix** well with the other children at the party.

MONDAY

Monday is the second day of the week, the day after Sunday.

MONEY

Coins and banknotes are **money**. We buy things with **money**.
Daffy Duck keeps her **money** in her handbag.

MONKEY

A **monkey** is a small animal which lives in trees. Mickey **Monkey** has a long tail and his hands look somewhat like ours.

MONTH

A **month** is a period of time. The year is divided into twelve **months**. They are January, February, March, April, May, June, July, August, September, October, November and December.

MOON

We see the **moon** in the sky at night.
The **moon** moves round the Earth every 29½ days. Sometimes we see all of one side of it; sometimes we only see part of one side. We never see the far side of the **moon** from Earth.
The **moon** appears to shine because it reflects the light of the sun.

MOP

A **mop** is a tool for cleaning floors. A **mop** has a sponge, or twists of wool or rags, fastened to a long handle.

MORE

More means greater in number or amount.
2 x 10 is **more** than 2 x 5.
A mile is **more** than a kilometre.
Piggles Pig eats **more** than Billy Budgie does.

MORNING

Morning is the first half of the day ending at noon.
What time do you get up in the **morning**?

MOSQUITO

A **mosquito** is a small, two-winged flying insect. The female can transmit a serious illness called malaria.

MOSS

Moss is a tiny, ground-hugging green plant that grows in tight clusters on moist ground, rocks and trees. Some birds line their nests with **moss** because it is very soft.

MOST

Most means the greatest in number, amount or degree.
Most children like sweets.
Bobby Boy scored the **most** goals.
Ossie Ostrich's foot is **most** painful.

MOTHER

A **mother** is a female parent.
To **mother** is to take care of.
Natalie Niece likes to **mother** Bouncing Baby.

MOTOR

A **motor** is a machine that makes things move.
This lawn-mower is run by a petrol **motor**.

MOUNT

To **mount** is to go up or to get up on something.
Dad will **mount** the ladder to mend the roof.
Baby Brother **mounted** Hobby Horse and had a long ride.

MOUNTAIN

A **mountain** is a very high hill. Some **mountains** are so tall that their peaks are always covered in snow.

MOUSE

A **mouse** is a small animal with grey, brown or white fur that lives in the fields and woods or in houses. Missy **Mouse** has a pointed nose and a long, thin tail.

MOUTH

The **mouth** is an opening in the face through which we speak and eat and can also breathe.
Leo Lion has sharp teeth in his **mouth**.
Frankie Frog has a long tongue in his **mouth**.

MOVE

To **move** is to go from one place to another or to put something in a different place.

Stand still! Don't **move** till I say, "Go! ".

Please **move** your coat from the chair.

MOW

To **mow** is to cut down.

Dad will **mow** the lawn.

MUCH

Much means a large quantity or amount.

There was **much** laughter at the circus.

How **much** ice-cream did you buy?

Don't eat too **much**.

MUD

Mud is soft, wet, sticky earth.

Please wipe the **mud** off your boots.

MUG

A **mug** is a tall cup with a handle.

We drink liquids from **mugs**.

MULE

A **mule** is an animal which is half donkey and half horse.

A **mule** can carry very heavy loads.

MULTIPLY

To **multiply** is to increase in number.

Daisies **multiply** from year to year.

In arithmetic, to **multiply** is to add a number to itself a set number of times.

Two **multiplied** by five equals ten.

$2 \times 5 = 2+2+2+2+2 = 10$.

MUSEUM

A **museum** is a building where collections of valuable and interesting things are on show.

There was a huge skeleton of a dinosaur at the **museum**.

MUSHROOM

A **mushroom** is a fungus that grows very quickly and is good to eat.

Mushy **Mushroom** is shaped like an umbrella.

MUSIC

Music is sound that is pleasing to hear.

We make **music** when we sing or when we play **musical** instruments.

MUST

Must means that you have to or ought to do a certain thing.

Bobby Boy **must** feed Digger Dog every day.

You **must** keep away from dangerous places and dangerous things.

MYSTERY

A **mystery** is something strange that is not easily explained or understood.

Nn

NAIL

A **nail** is a thin, sharp, pointed piece of metal used to join things. Farmer Brown fastens his wooden fences together with **nails**. You also have a **nail** at the end of each of your fingers and toes.

NAME

What is your **name**? What are you called?
The dog's **name** is Digger. We call the dog Digger.

NAP

If you are tired during the day you take a **nap**. You have a short sleep. Baby Brother has a **nap** after lunch.

NAPKIN

A **napkin** is made of cloth or paper. It protects our clothes when we eat.
Nancy **Napkin** is made of linen.

NARROW

The stripes on Benjamin Butcher's apron are **narrow**.
They are not wide.

NATIVE

Zebby Zebra is a **native** of Africa. That is where he comes from.

NATURE

Anything in our world not made by man is part of **nature**.
The sea, sky, mountains, animals, birds and trees are all part of **nature**. They are **natural**.

NAUGHTY

Clarence Cat was **naughty** today. He was not good. He stole a fish from the table.

NAVY

The fleet of ships and all the people serving on them make up a country's **navy**.

NEAR

Nice Nurse lives **near** the hospital. She lives close to the hospital.

NEAT

Jenny keeps her room **neat**. She keeps it clean and tidy.

NECESSARY

Something that must be had or done is **necessary**.
It is **necessary** for Gilly Goldfish to have water in her bowl so that she can breathe.
She must have water in her bowl.

NECK

Your **neck** is the part of your body between your head and shoulders.
George Giraffe's **neck** is very long.

NECKLACE

A string of beads worn round the neck is a **necklace**.
Aunty Ivy wears a pearl **necklace**.

NEED

We **need** to eat to give us energy.
We must eat.
Andy Ambulance **needs** a siren.
He has to have a siren.

NEEDLE

A **needle** is a thin piece of metal with a point at one end and a hole at the other to hold thread.
Belinda Ballerina uses a **needle** to sew the sequins on to her dress.

NEIGHBOUR

Mary lives next door to Joe.
She is Joe's **neighbour**.

NEITHER

Neither means not one and not the other of two.
Neither Jenny nor Jill is a boy.
They are both girls.

NEPHEW

Someone's **nephew** is the child of that person's brother or sister.
My **nephew**, Shaun, is my sister's son.
My **nephew**, Peter, is my brother's son.

NERVOUS

Missy Mouse is **nervous** of Clarence Cat.
She is afraid of Clarence Cat.

NEST

The bird built a **nest** in the tree.
This is its home.
It will lay its eggs in its **nest**.

NET

A **net** can be made of string or wire.
Farmer Brown has a wire **net** round his field.
When we play tennis we hit the ball to and fro over the **net**.

NEVER

Tilly Tortoise will **never** run as fast as Digger Dog.
At no time will she be able to run as fast as Digger Dog.

NEW

Baby Brother has a **new** toy.
It is not old: Mummy has just bought it from the shop.
Aunty Ivy has a **new** hairstyle.
She has a different hairstyle.

NEWSPAPER

News is printed in a **newspaper**. Tommy Teacher reads his **newspaper** each morning before going to school.

NINE

Nine is a number.
Nine is one more than eight.
If you add 5 and 4 you have **9**.

NINETEEN

Nineteen is a number.
Nineteen is one more than eighteen.
If you add 10 and 9 you have **19**.

NEXT

Big Bus is parked **next** to Minnie Mini-Bus. They are side by side. Big Bus will be the **next** bus to leave the bus station. No other bus will go before he does.

NIGHT

Night is the dark time of day after sunset.
We go to bed at **night**.
The stars come out at **night**.

NO

No is used to answer a question to show that you do not agree with something.
Is Elly Elephant small? **No**, she is large.

NICE

Daniel Dwarf is a **nice** man. He is a likeable man.
Jack and Jill had a **nice** time at the zoo. They had a very pleasant time at the zoo.

NIGHTDRESS

Belinda Ballerina wears a pretty **nightdress** when she goes to bed. Baby Brother wears pyjamas.

NOBODY

Nobody means no-one.
Big Bus has no passengers. There is **nobody** on the bus.

NONE

None means not one.
Bobby Boy had eaten all the sweets. There were **none** left.

NOON

Noon is 12 o'clock in the middle of the day. The sun is at its highest at **noon**.
We eat lunch at **noon**.

NIECE

Someone's **niece** is the daughter of that person's brother or sister.
My **niece**, Sharon, is my brother's daughter.
My **niece**, Julie, is my sister's daughter.

NOT

Not means to deny or refuse.
Albert Ape will **not** wash his jeans.
He refuses to wash them.

NOTE

John wrote Jane a **note**.
He wrote her a short letter.
Bobby Boy played a **note** on the piano. He struck a key and made it sound.

NOTHING

There is **nothing** left in Digger Dog's bowl.
It is empty. He has eaten everything.

NOTICE

Did you **notice** Clarence Cat's sharp claws? Did you see them?
Tommy Teacher pinned a **notice** on the wall. He wrote a message on a card and put it on the wall.

NOUGHT

Nought is the figure **0**.
If you take 5 away from 5 you have **0**.

NOVEMBER

November is the eleventh month of the year.
November has thirty days.

NOW

Now means at this moment.
I am reading this book **now**.

NUMBER

A **number** is a figure not a letter and it tells you how much or how many of something.
Elly Elephant has 4 legs. 4 is the **number** of legs she has.

NURSE

A **nurse** looks after people when they are ill.
Nice **Nurse** looks after people in hospital.

NURSERY

Small children are looked after in a **nursery**.
Young plants are grown in a **nursery**.

NYLON

Nylon is a strong, man-made material.
Aunty Ivy's stockings are made of **nylon**.

OAK

An **oak** is a type of tree.
The wood from **oak** trees is hard.
Acorns grow on **oak** trees.

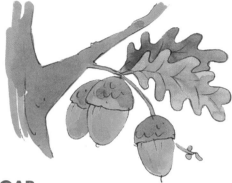

OAR

An **oar** is a flat blade of wood with a long handle. A boat can be rowed with two **oars**.

OATS

Farmer Brown grows **oats** on his farm.
When they are ripe he harvests them.
Filly Foal likes to eat **oats**.
We eat **oatmeal** made from **oats**.

OBEY

You should **obey** your parents and your teacher.
You should do what they tell you to.

OBJECT

An **object** is a thing. This book is an **object**.
Missy Mouse **objects** if Clarence Cat chases her. She does not like it.

OBLONG

An **oblong** is a shape which is longer than it is wide.
Some loaves of bread are **oblong-shaped**. Bricks are also **oblong**.

OCCASION

An **occasion** is a happening or an event.
A birthday is a special **occasion**.

OCEAN

An **ocean** is a large area of salt water. There are five **oceans** altogether. The Atlantic **Ocean** is one. Do you know the others?

O'CLOCK

O'clock is used in telling the time say what hour it is.
Four **o'clock** is tea time.
Nine **o'clock** is the time school begins.

OCTOBER

October is the tenth month of the year.
There are thirty-one days in **October**.

OCTOPUS

An **octopus** lives in the sea. It has eight long arms, or tentacles, with suckers which it uses to catch its food.

OF

Of means belonging to or made from.
Nancy Napkin is made **of** linen.
Mother Goose is the mother **of** many children.

OFF

Off has several meanings.
The light is **off**. It is not working.
Baby Brother fell **off** his chair.
He fell to the floor.

OFFICE

An **office** is a room or building where business is carried out.
Dad has a desk and a telephone in his **office**.

OFTEN

Gilly Goldfish **often** swims round her bowl.
She swims round her bowl many times.

OIL

There are many kinds of **oil**.
Oil is a very important liquid fuel for industry.
It is used to make engines run smoothly.
Olive **oil** is used for cooking.

OLD

Mother Goose is **old**. She is not young.
Arnold Aircraft is **old**. He is not new.

OMELETTE

An **omelette** is a kind of pancake.
When Henrietta Hen lays some eggs we can use them to make an **omelette**.

ON

This word can tell you where things are or it can mean the opposite of off.
Digger Dog is sleeping **on** the settee.
Brian Baker must switch **on** the oven before he can bake his bread.

ONCE

Once means one time only.
Bobby Boy missed the school bus **once**. He missed it on one occasion only.

ONE

One is the first number. If you take 2 from 3 you have **1**.

ONION

An **onion** is a vegetable. It has a strong smell.
Chief Chef puts an **onion** in his casserole.

ONLY

Belinda Ballerina is an **only** child. She has no brothers or sisters.
Natalie Niece had **only** a sandwich for lunch. She had nothing else to eat for lunch.

OPEN

Nellie Neighbour's window is **open**. It is not shut.
Benjamin Butcher's shop is **open**. It is ready for the customers to come in.

OPERA

An **opera** is a play in which the words are sung instead of spoken. Perhaps Carol Canary could sing in **opera**.

OPPOSITE

Opposite means as different as possible or helps to tell you where something is.

Wet is the **opposite** of dry.
Fast is the **opposite** of slow.
The toyshop is **opposite** the post office.

OR

Or shows that there is a choice.
Leo Lion can wear his red shorts **or** his blue shorts. He can wear either.

ORANGE

An **orange** is a juicy, round fruit that grows in hot countries. It is very good to eat.
Orange is a colour between red and yellow.

ORANG-UTAN

An **orang-utan** is a large ape from Borneo or Sumatra which lives in trees. **Orang-utans** have long arms, short legs and are covered in reddish-brown hair.

ORCHARD

Fruit trees grow in an **orchard**. Farmer Brown has a small field of apple, pear and plum trees. This is his **orchard**.

ORCHESTRA

An **orchestra** is a group of people who play music together. Lots of different instruments make up an **orchestra**.

ORGAN

An **organ** is a very large, musical instrument, often found in a church. It has keys rather like a piano.

ORPHAN

Norman Nephew is an **orphan**. Both his mother and father have died.

OSTRICH

Ossie is an **ostrich**. He is a large bird from Africa. He can run very fast but he cannot fly.

OTHER

Are there any **other** passengers waiting for Big Bus?
Are there any more passengers waiting for Big Bus?
I will go home by the **other** road.
I will take a different way home.

OTTER

An **otter** is an animal which lives by rivers or lakes.
An **otter** swims very well and feeds on fish.

OUR

Our means belonging to us. Jenny and I share a room. It is **our** room.

OUT

Mother Goose is **out**. She is not at home.
The light is **out**. It is no longer lit.

OUTDOOR

Outdoor means in the open air. Football and rugby are **outdoor** games.

OUTSIDE

The dog's kennel is **outside** the house. It is not inside.

OVAL

Oval is a shape.
An egg is **oval**.
A rugby ball is **oval**.

OVEN

The **oven** is the part of the cooker used for baking and roasting.
Brian Baker bakes bread in his **oven**.

OVER

Over can mean above, covering or finished.
Kathy Kangaroo jumped **over** the fence.
Natalie Niece often wears a sweater **over** her blouse.
The game was **over**. It had finished.

OWE

Jack **owes** Jill fifty pence. He has borrowed the money from Jill and must pay it back.

OWL

An **owl** is a bird. An **owl** has big eyes and flies mostly at night.

OWN

To **own** something is to have or possess something.
Farmer Brown **owns** his farm. It is his property.

OX

An **ox** is a large, farm animal. In some countries **oxen** are used for pulling carts or ploughs.

OYSTER

An **oyster** is a type of shellfish.
The shell of an **oyster** may contain a pearl.

Pp

PACK

A group of wolves is called a **pack** of wolves.
Nellie Neighbour **packs** her clothes when she goes on holiday.
She puts them all in a bag.

PAD

A **pad** can be a cushion.
Bouncing Baby has a **pad** on his bed to make it soft.
Several sheets of paper fastened together make a different kind of **pad**.

PADDLE

People **paddle** in the sea when they are on holiday.
They walk in shallow water.
A **paddle** is a short pole with a flat end which is used to move a canoe through the water.

PAGE

A **page** is a sheet of paper in a book or a magazine.
This book contains lots of **pages**.

PAIL

Farmer Brown carries water to his animals in a **pail**.
He fills a bucket with water and takes it to his animals.

PAIN

Uncle Harry has a **pain** in his head.
His head hurts. It is **painful**.

PAINT

Nellie Neighbour is going to **paint** her door green.
She will colour her door with a green liquid.

PAIR

A **pair** is two things of the same kind.
Bobby Boy has a **pair** of black shoes.
Bouncing Baby has a **pair** of white mittens.

PALACE

The Queen lives in a **palace**.
It is a large and splendid house with many rooms.

PALE

Pale means light-coloured or not bright.
Uncle Harry's face was **pale** when he was not well.

PALM

The **palm** of your hand is the inside of your hand.
You can hold small items in the **palm** of your hand.

PAN

A **pan** is a metal container used for cooking.
Chief Chef uses a lot of **pans** when he is working.

PANCAKE

A pancake is good to eat.
It is made from flour, milk and eggs
and is cooked in a frying pan.

PANDA

A panda is a large animal rather
like a bear.
The giant panda is black and white
and comes from China.

PANTOMIME

A pantomime is usually
performed at Christmas-time. It is a
play which tells a fairy story.
Cinderella is my favourite
pantomime.

PAPER

Paper is used to write on. Exercise
books are made of paper.
This book is made of paper.

PARACHUTE

Uncle Harry used a parachute
when he jumped from Arnold
Aircraft.
A parachute was fastened to his
body and when it opened he floated
to the ground.

PARADE

Jack and Jill marched in the
parade.
A band played music and lots of
people paraded through the town.

PARCEL

The postman brought the boy a big
parcel on his birthday. He brought
a package wrapped in paper and
tied with string.

PARENT

A father is a parent.
A mother is a parent.
Jack and Jill have the same
parents so they are brother and
sister.

PARK

A park is a large public garden in
a town.
There are sometimes slides in the
park.

PARROT

Natalie Niece has a parrot for a
pet. A parrot
is a bird
which has
beautiful,
brightly-
coloured
feathers
and a
curved
beak.

PART

A part is a section or piece of
something. Bobby Boy did not eat all
the cake. He only ate part of it.

PARTY

Bobby Boy had a party on his
birthday. He invited his friends to his
house and they played games and
had nice things to eat.
He had a birthday party.

PASS

Minnie Mini-Bus will **pass** Big Bus on the road.
Minnie Mini-Bus will go faster and go by Big Bus.

PASSENGER

A **passenger** travels in a vehicle. Big Bus carries lots of **passengers**.

PAST

Bouncing Baby should be asleep now. It is **past** his bedtime. It is after his bedtime.
Caw-Caw Crow flew **past** the window.
He flew by the window.

PASTE

Jack and Jill **paste** pictures in their scrapbooks. They stick the pictures in their books.

PASTRY

Pastry is used to make pies or flans. It is a mixture of flour, fat, water and salt.
Brian Baker mixes lots of **pastry** to bake into delicious pies.

PAT

Bobby Boy wants to **pat** Digger Dog.
He wants to tap him gently with his hand to show affection.

PATH

Jack and Jill walked on the **path** through the park. Cars are not allowed on the **path**. It is only used for walking on.

PATIENT

Nice Nurse cares for **patients** in her hospital. She looks after people who are sick.

PATTERN

Nellie Neighbour made a dress using a **pattern**. She used the **pattern** as a guide. She likes the pretty **pattern** on her material. She likes the design

PAW

A **paw** is the foot of an animal. It has claws on it.
Digger Dog and Clarence Cat each have four **paws**.

PAY

Nellie Neighbour must **pay** Benjamin Butcher when she buys her meat from his shop. She must give him money in exchange for the meat.

PEA

Farmer Brown grows **peas** on his farm.
Pea seeds are round and green and good to eat. They grow in pods on the **pea** plant.

PEACE

A quiet time when there is no fighting or war is called **peace**. It is **peaceful** when Bouncing Baby stops crying and goes to sleep.

PEACH

Belinda Ballerina ate a **peach**. She ate a juicy, round fruit with a yellowish-red skin.

PEACOCK

A **peacock** is a large bird. It has a large tail of beautiful colours which it can spread out like a fan.

PEAR

A **pear** is good to eat. It is a type of fruit and is wider at the bottom than the top.

PEARL

A **pearl** is a small, round, valuable stone found in some oyster shells. It is used in jewellery. Aunty Ivy has a **pearl** necklace.

PEBBLE

A **pebble** is a small stone. Bobby Boy collected some **pebbles** on the beach and used them to decorate his sandcastle.

PEDESTRIAN

When Jenny walks down the street she is a **pedestrian**. She must cross the road at a **pedestrian-crossing**. She must cross at a special place for people on foot.

PEEL

Albert Ape must **peel** the banana before he eats it. He must take the skin off.

PEG

Jenny uses a **peg** to fasten her washing to the line. Tommy Teacher hangs his cloak on a **peg** behind the door.

PELICAN

A **pelican** is a large water-fowl. It has a huge pouch on its lower bill which will hold many fish at a time.

PEN

Aunty Ivy writes a letter with her **pen**. She writes using ink. Farmer Brown keeps his sheep in a **pen**. He keeps them in a yard with a fence round it.

PENCIL

Bobby Boy draws with a **pencil**. Sometimes he uses a **pencil** with lead in it and sometimes he uses a coloured **pencil**.

PENGUIN

Peter **Penguin** lives near the South Pole. He is a black and white bird who lives near the water. **Penguins** cannot fly. They swim well and eat fish.

PEOPLE

Big Bus carries lots of **people** on his journeys. He carries men, women and children.

PEPPER

Pepper is used for flavouring food. It tastes hot.
Mother adds some **pepper** to the stew to give it more flavour.

PERFUME

The roses in Aunty Ivy's garden have a pleasant **perfume**. They smell good.

PERHAPS

Perhaps means possibly or maybe.
Perhaps Clarence Cat will catch a mouse. Clarence Cat might catch a mouse.

PERMISSION

Brian Baker gave Jenny **permission** to take a cake. He allowed her to take a cake.

PERSON

Benjamin Butcher is a **person**. Nellie Neighbour is a **person**. A **person** is a human being.

PHOTOGRAPH

Photographs are pictures taken with a camera. People often take **photographs** of each other.

PIANO

A **piano** is a large musical instrument with a keyboard. Do you have a **piano** at your home?

PICTURE

Bobby Boy drew a **picture** of Digger Dog. He drew a likeness of Digger Dog.
Aunty Ivy has lots of **pictures** on her walls.

PIECE

Bobby Boy eats a **piece** of cake. He eats a part of the cake.

PIG

Piggles **Pig** lives in a sty on Farmer Brown's farm. He has four short legs and a curly tail.
Ham and pork come from **pigs**.

PIGEON

A **pigeon** is a type of bird.
Pigeons can be trained to carry messages tied to their legs.

PILE

A heap of things on top of each other is a **pile**.
Basil Builder has a **pile** of bricks in his yard.

PILL

Doc Doctor gave Mother a **pill** when she was not well. He gave her medicine in a tiny, solid ball which she swallowed.

PILLOW

A **pillow** is a type of of cushion for the head.
Aunty Ivy has a soft **pillow** on her bed.

PILOT

A **pilot** is the person in charge of flying an aircraft.
A ship's **pilot** guides ships in and out of harbours.

PIPE

A **pipe** is a hollow tube.
Water runs into houses and to taps through **pipes**. Gas is also carried through **pipes**.

PITCH

Football is played on a **pitch**. It is a playing field for sports.
Another kind of **pitch** is a black, sticky substance obtained from tar.

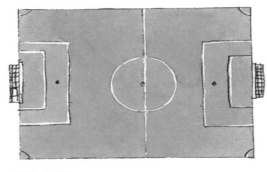

PLACE

A particular area is a **place**.
An office is a **place** of work. School is a **place** to learn.

PLANT

Any living thing which grows that is not an animal, bird or insect is a **plant**.
Vegetables, flowers, bushes and trees are **plants**.

PLAYGROUND

There is a large **playground** at Tommy Teacher's school.
A **playground** is a place where children can play. Sometimes there are swings and slides in a **playground**.

PLUMBER

When Nellie Neighbour's tap began to drip she called a **plumber**.
A **plumber** mends and installs water systems.

POCKET

Nice Nurse has a **pocket** in her uniform. She has a type of bag sewn into her uniform. She keeps her handkerchief in her **pocket**.

POEM

Can you write a **poem**?
A **poem** is a piece of writing usually in rhyme.

PONY

A **pony** is a small horse.
Farmer Brown has a **pony** for the children to ride.

POTATO

A **potato** is a vegetable which grows below the ground.
We make chips from **potatoes**.

PRAWN

A **prawn** is a type of shellfish and lives in water.
Do you like **prawn** cocktail?

PRESENT

A **present** is a gift.
Belinda Ballerina received lots of **presents** on her birthday.

PRICE

What is the **price** of that bicycle in the shop window? How much does it cost?
The **price** of something is the amount of money it costs.

PROMISE

To **promise** is to say you will do something and to do it.
Bobby Boy **promised** to tidy his own room so he had to do it.

PUPIL

A **pupil** is somebody who is being taught.
Tommy Teacher has lots of **pupils** at his school.

PURSE

Aunty Ivy keeps her money in a **purse**.
A **purse** is a small bag for carrying money.

PUSH

To **push** is to use force to move something forward.
Mother has to **push** Bouncing Baby's pram to make it move.

PUT

Nice Nurse will **put** a vase of flowers on the patient's table.
She will place a vase of flowers on the table.

PYJAMAS

Do you wear **pyjamas** to sleep in?
Bobby Boy is wearing his **pyjamas**. He has a thin jacket and trousers, of the same material, to wear in bed.

Qq

QUACK
"Quack!" is what Daffy Duck says.
Quacking is the sound made by ducks.

QUARREL
John and Jane had a quarrel.
They had an argument.

QUARTER
A quarter is one of four equal parts of anything.
Brian Baker cut the cake into four equal parts.
He cut it into quarters.

QUEEN
A queen is a woman who rules over a country.
The wife of a king is called a queen.

QUESTION
How old are you? That is a question.
A question asks for information.

QUEUE
There is a queue at Benjamin Butcher's shop. There is a line of people waiting to be served.

QUICK
Nellie Neighbour must be quick if she wants to catch the bus.
She must hurry.

QUIET
Bobby Boy must be quiet or he will wake Bouncing Baby.

QUILT
Uncle Harry has a quilt on his bed. He has a padded covering which keeps him warm.

QUIT
To quit is to stop or give up.
Naughty Norman Nephew quit school.
He stopped going to school.

QUITE
Brian Baker's cakes are quite delicious. They are really delicious.
Baby Brother has been quite good today. He has been really good.

QUIZ
Tommy Teacher organised a quiz at school. He held a competition and asked his pupils questions.

103

Rr

RABBIT
A **rabbit** is a small animal with soft fur. Reginald **Rabbit** has long ears and lives in a burrow.

RACE
A **race** is a competition to see who can go the fastest.
You can have **races** on foot, or car, horse and bicycle **races**.

RADIO
Aunty Ivy likes listening to music on her **radio**.
A **radio** is a piece of equipment for sending and receiving sound waves.

RAG
Mother cleans her oven with a **rag**.
She uses a piece of old cloth.

RAIL

A **rail** is a bar of wood or metal. Farmer Brown has a wooden **rail** fence around his fields.
Tracy Train runs on steel **rails**.

RAIN

Mother Goose hopes it will not **rain** today because she has hung her washing out to dry.
When it **rains** drops of water fall from the clouds.

RAINBOW
A **rainbow** appears in the sky when the sun shines through rain.
A **rainbow** is an arch of seven colours and is very pretty.

RAINCOAT
Uncle Harry will wear his **raincoat** because it is raining. He will not get wet because a **raincoat** is a waterproof coat.

RAISE
Tommy Teacher told the children to **raise** their hands if they knew the answer to his question.
He told them to lift up their hands.

RAKE
A **rake** is a long-handled, gardening tool for gathering up leaves or grass.

RAT

Raymond **Rat** looks like a large mouse. A **rat** is an animal with a long tail and sharp teeth.

RATHER
Bobby Boy would **rather** watch television than go to bed. He prefers to watch television.
It is **rather** cold today.
It is quite cold today.

RAVEN

A **raven** is a large, black bird with a sharp beak. A **raven** looks like a crow but it is much bigger.

RAW

Benjamin Butcher sells **raw** meat in his shop. He sells meat that is not cooked.
Most fruit can be eaten **raw**.

REACH

Big Bus will **reach** the terminus at midday.
He will arrive at the terminus at midday.
Bobby Boy tries to **reach** the top shelf.
He stretches out his arms to touch the shelf.

READ

To **read** is to look at words and understand what they mean.
You are **reading** this book.

READY

Dinner is **ready**. Dinner is cooked and on the table or prepared for you to eat.
Nellie Neighbour is **ready** to go out.
She has her coat on and is about to go out.

REAL

Real means true and not imagined. Digger Dog is a **real** dog. He is a proper dog and not a toy.

REAR

Uncle Harry sat at the **rear** of the bus.
He sat at the back of the bus.

REASON

Nice Nurse was late for work because she missed the bus.
That is the **reason** she was late.

RECEIVE

Bobby boy is happy to **receive** a present on his birthday.
To **receive** is to accept something that is given.

RECOGNISE

Benjamin Butcher will **recognise** his regular customers. He will know them because he has seen them before.

RECTANGLE

A **rectangle** is a shape with four straight sides of two different lengths. All the corners of a **rectangle** are always right angles. Tommy Teacher has drawn a **rectangle** on the blackboard.

RED

Red is a colour. Some apples are **red**. Do you like **red** apples or green apples?

REFEREE

The **referee** is the person in charge of a game. He **referees** the game and makes sure that the rules of the game are obeyed.

REFRIGERATOR

Food and drink are stored in a **refrigerator** to keep them cool and fresh.
A **refrigerator** can run on either gas or electricity.

REINDEER

Roland **Reindeer** is a large deer with long, branching horns.
Reindeer come from the cold lands of the North.
How many **reindeer** does Santa Claus have?

REMAIN

Baby Brother must **remain** at home. He must stay at home because he has a bad cold.

REMEMBER

Remember to take your books to school in the morning.
Do not forget them.
Did you **remember** to clean your teeth this morning?

REMOVE

Farmer Brown must **remove** his muddy boots before he goes into the house. He must take them off.

RENT

Nellie Neighbour pays **rent** for the use of her house.
She pays money to the person who owns her house.

REPAIR

When Big Bus broke down he had to go to the garage for **repair**.
He had to go to the garage to be mended.

REPORT

We heard a **report** on the radio about the football match. The **reporter** described what happened at the game.

REPTILE

A **reptile** is a cold-blooded animal with scales. Ally Alligator and Christopher Crocodile are **reptiles**.

REQUEST

Norman Nephew **requests** an ice-cream.
He asks politely for an ice-cream.

REST

After work Dad likes to have a **rest**.
He sits down and relaxes.
Bobby Boy will watch the **rest** of the match. He will watch the remainder of the match.

RESTAURANT

A **restaurant** is a place where meals are served.
Chief Chef cooks meals in a **restaurant**.

RETURN

You must **return** to school on Monday after the weekend break.
You must go back to school on Monday.

RHINOCEROS

A **rhinoceros** is a large animal with a thick skin. **Rhinoceroses** come from Africa or Asia.
Ronnie **Rhinoceros** has one horn on his nose but others may have two.

RICH

Farmer Brown is **rich.** He has lots of money.
If you saved all your pocket-money you would be **rich** too.

RIDE

Bobby Boy can **ride** a bicycle. He can travel along without falling off. You can also **ride** on a horse or **ride** in a bus.

RIGHT

Do you know the **right** answer?
Do you know the correct answer?
Jack writes with his **right** hand but Jill writes with her left hand.

RING

Nellie Neighbour wears a **ring** on her finger. The **ring** is a circle of gold.
Did you hear the bell **ring**? Did you hear the sound of the bell?

RIPE

The banana is **ripe**. It is not green but yellow and ready to eat.

RISE

The sun will **rise** in the sky. It will come up in the sky.

RIVER

A **river** is a stream of water which flows into the sea or into another **river**.
Uncle Harry likes to fish in the **river**.

ROAD

Big Bus travels along the **road**.
A **road** is a hard surface especially made for vehicles to travel on.

ROAR

Leo Lion and Tiggy Tiger **roar**.
A **roar** is a deep, loud sound.

ROAST

Granny **roasts** meat in the oven.
She cooks it in the oven.
Do you prefer **roast** beef or **roast** chicken for dinner?

ROBIN

A **robin** is a small, brown bird with a red breast.
Look at Red **Robin** sitting on Dad's spade.

ROCK

A **rock** is a piece of stone.
Another kind of **rock** is a hard, long sweet. Perhaps you have bought some **rock** at the seaside.

ROLL

Digger Dog likes to **roll** in the grass. He turns over and over.
Brian Baker makes bread **rolls**. He makes bread in small round shapes.

ROOF

A **roof** covers the top of a building. It keeps the rain out.
Farmer Brown's barn has a **roof** made of green tiles.

ROOM

A **room** is a part of a building with its own walls, ceiling, floor and door. How many **rooms** does your house have?

ROOT

All plants have **roots**. The **root** is the part which grows under the ground. Water is taken in through the **roots**.

ROPE

A **rope** is a thick string.
Farmer Brown ties a **rope** to Gertie Goat's collar to lead her to the field.

ROSE

A **rose** is a pretty flower which grows on a bush. **Roses** have thorns on their stems.

ROTTEN

The apples at the bottom of the barrel were **rotten**.
They had gone bad and were not fit to eat.

ROUGH

The sea is **rough** today. It is not calm.
Elly Elephant's skin is **rough**. It is not smooth.

ROUND

Round means shaped like a ball or a circle. **Round** things roll easily.

ROUTE

When we go on holiday, Dad plans our **route** very carefully. He plans which roads we should take.

ROW

Uncle Harry planted a **row** of potatoes in his garden. He planted them in a neat line.
Dad **rows** his boat across the river. He moves it along with the oars.

RUB

To slide something backwards and forwards against something else is to **rub**.
Dad **rubs** his hands together to warm them when he is cold.

RUBBER

Rubber is made from the sap of a tropical tree. Lots of things are made of **rubber**, for example tyres and erasers.

RUBBISH

Rubbish is waste material or unwanted things.
We throw **rubbish** into a dustbin.

RUDE

Bobby Boy was **rude** to his mother. It is bad-mannered to be **rude** to others.

RUG

A **rug** is a cover for part of the floor.
Aunty Ivy has a pretty **rug** beside her bed.

RULE

A **rule** tells you what you should or should not do.
At school you must not talk in assembly. That is a **rule**.

RUN

When you **run** you move with much quicker steps than you do when you walk.
Jack can **run** faster than Jill.

RUNWAY

A **runway** is a level strip of land especially for the use of aeroplanes. Arnold Aircraft takes off and lands on a **runway**.

RUSH

To **rush** means to hurry. The children **rush** home from school so that they can go out to play.

RYE

Rye is a grain which is used for feeding to animals.
Whisky and bread can also be made from **rye**.

Ss

SACK

A **sack** is a large bag in which we carry things.
Farmer Brown is carrying a **sack** of corn.
Chief Chef bought a **sack** of potatoes.

SADDLE

A **saddle** is a seat.
We sit on a **saddle** when we go for a ride on a horse or a bicycle.

SAFE

Safe means free from harm or danger.
You are **safe** when a policeman helps you cross the street.

SALT

Salt is a white, grainy substance found in the ground and in sea water.
We sprinkle **salt** on food to make it taste better.

SAME

Same means just like.
Bobby Boy's ball is the **same** as Baby Brother's ball.
It is the **same** size and the **same** colour.

SAND

Sand is tiny grains of worn-down rock found on the seashore or in deserts.
Baby Brother likes to play in the **sand** on the seashore.

SATCHEL

A **satchel** is a small bag.
Bobby Boy carries his books in a **satchel** when he goes to school.

SATURDAY

Saturday is the seventh day of the week.
Saturday comes after Friday.

SAVE

When you **save** your pocket money you keep it to spend later.
Firemen often **save** people from danger.
They rescue people from burning buildings.

SAW

A **saw** is a tool for cutting wood and metal.
A **saw** has a thin, metal blade with sharp teeth.
Norman Nephew used a **saw** to cut down an old tree.

SAY

Say means to speak or tell or put something in words.
We usually **say** 'Goodnight' when we go to bed.
This dictionary **says** that a satchel is a small bag.

SCALE

A **scale** is a machine for weighing things.
Bobby Boy stands on the **scales** to weigh himself.
A **scale** is also one of the thin, hard flakes covering the skin of snakes, lizards and some fishes.
A **scale** is also a run of notes in music.

SCARF

A **scarf** is a long strip of cloth worn round the neck or shoulders or round the head.
Mother knitted a warm, woollen **scarf** for Bouncing Baby.

SCHOOL

School is a place for teaching and learning.
Children go to **school** to learn.
Tommy Teacher teaches the pupils at his **school**.

SCISSORS

Scissors have two sharp blades that are fastened in the middle. We use **scissors** to cut paper and cloth.
Barry Barber cuts Baby Brother's hair with **scissors**.

SCREAM

We **scream** when we are in pain or get a fright.
Baby Brother **screamed** when he fell and hurt his leg.
Would you **scream** if you saw a ghost?

SEA

The **sea** is salt water that covers a large part of the earth's surface.
Wally Whale and Flipper Fish swim in the **sea**.

SEAL

Sammy **Seal** is a sea animal with furry skin. **Seals** have flippers to help them swim.

SEASON

A **season** is one quarter of a year. Spring, summer, autumn and winter are the four **seasons** of the year.

SEAT

A **seat** is a thing to sit on.
Chairs, stools, benches and sofas are all **seats**.

SECOND

The **second** is the one after the first.
Elly Elephant came first in the race and Daniel Dwarf came **second**.
A **second** is also a short period of time. There are sixty **seconds** in a minute.

SECRET

A **secret** is something only you know until you choose to tell other people about it.
Digger Dog hides his bones in a **secret** place.

SEE

We **see** with our eyes.
What do you see on this page?
Eric Elf went to **see** Daniel Dwarf last Saturday. He went to visit him.

SEED

A **seed** is that part of a plant which can grow into another plant.
Aunty Ivy plants **seeds** in her garden.
Farmer Brown plants grass and vegetable **seeds** in his fields.

SELL

If you **sell** something you hand it over in exchange for money.
Benjamin Butcher **sells** meat.
Brian Baker **sells** bread and cakes.

SEND

To **send** is to cause something or someone to move from one place to another.
Bobby Boy will **send** Aunty Ivy a present at Christmas.
Mother will **send** Baby Brother to bed if he is ill and then she will **send** for the doctor.

SENTENCE

A **sentence** is a group of words that tell or ask something.
Can you read this **sentence**?
Sidney Ship sails on the sea.

SEPTEMBER

September is the ninth month of the year.
There are thirty days in **September**.

SERVE

Mother will **serve** the food.
She will wait on us and give us our share.

SET

Please **set** the room straight. Put everything in its proper place.
Doc Doctor can **set** a broken bone.
Mother Goose **set** the table for the party.
Bobby Boy **set** the alarm for seven o'clock.

SEVEN

Seven is the number after six.
Seven is one more than six.
There are **seven** days in a week.
$6 + 1 = 7$.

SEVENTEEN

Seventeen is the number after sixteen.
Seventeen is seven more than ten.
$10 + 7 = 17$.

SEW

To **sew** is to fasten cloth together with stitches.
We **sew** using a needle and thread. We can **sew** by hand or by using a **sewing** machine.

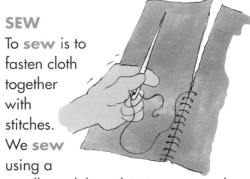

SHADOW

A **shadow** is a patch of shade. Anything blocking the light from the sun casts its own **shadow**. Wherever you go your **shadow** goes with you.

SHAKE

To **shake** something is to move it up and down, or from side to side, quickly.
The two boys **shake** the tree to get the apples.

SHALLOW

The water is **shallow**. It is not deep. It is usually safe to paddle in **shallow** water.

SHAMPOO

Mother will **shampoo** Bobby Boy's hair.
She will wash it with a mild **shampoo**.
Dad will **shampoo** the carpet after the party.

SHAPE

Every person and every thing has a **shape**.
The **shape** of a ball is round.
The **shape** of an egg is oval.
You might see the **shape** of a knight in a haunted castle.

SHARK

A **shark** is a large and dangerous fish with sharp teeth.
Sharks eat other fish and sometimes attack people swimming in the sea.

SHE

Belinda Ballerina is happy because **she** has a new dress.
Elly Elephant says **she** likes to dance.
She is the female person or animal spoken about.

SHEEP

A **sheep** is an animal with a thick woolly coat.
We get meat and wool from **sheep**.
Sheila **Sheep** is Lucy Lamb's mother.

SHELL

A **shell** is the hard, outside covering of some things.
An **eggshell** is easy to break.
A walnut **shell** is hard to break.
Tilly Tortoise has a hard **shell** on her back.

SHINE

To **shine** means to send or give out a steady light.
The moon will **shine** in the dark, clear sky.
We **shine** our shoes to make them clean and bright.

SHIP

A **ship** is a very large boat that sails on the sea.

SHIRT

A **shirt** is a garment worn on the upper part of the body.
Dad has a blue **shirt** with long sleeves but the boy has a red **shirt** with short sleeves.

SHOE

A **shoe** is a covering for the foot.
Most **shoes** are made of leather but some are made of cloth.
Shoes protect our feet.
A horse wears **shoes** made of iron.

SHOP

A **shop** is a place where we can buy things. When we **shop**, we visit **shops** to look at things we want to buy.
Bobby Boy bought a bunch of bananas from the fruit **shop**.

SHORE

The **shore** is the land at the edge of a sea or a lake.
The children have made a sand-castle on the **shore**.

SHORT

Short means not long or tall.
The boy has **short** hair but Natalie Niece has long hair.
Dad is tall but Baby Brother is **short**.

SHOULDER

A **shoulder** is the place where the arm of a person, or the front leg of an animal, joins the body.
Bobby Boy carries his satchel on his **shoulder**.

SHOW

Jack will **show** Jill the photograph he took of her. He will let her see it.
A **Show** can be a competition for animals or birds.
Digger Dog hopes to win a prize at the Dog **Show**.

SHUT

To **shut** is to close something. You **shut** your eyes when you go to sleep.
We **shut** doors, windows and gates.

SIGN

A **sign** is a mark or a note or an act that tells us something.
A shake of the fist is a **sign** of anger.
The **sign** on the gate says, 'Beware of the Bull'.
What do these signs mean? + − x ÷

SILENT

You are **silent** if you do not speak or make a sound.
Tommy Teacher asked the children to be **silent** while he showed them how to plant seeds.

SINCE

Since means from then until now.
Bobby Boy lost his ball on Saturday and has been unhappy ever **since**.
Since also means because.
Since it is raining you should take an umbrella.

SING

When you **sing** you make music with your voice.
Some people **sing** carols at Christmas. Most people can **sing** the 'Happy Birthday' song.
Carol Canary can **sing** sweetly.

SINK

A **sink** is a basin fitted with a drain.
We wash dishes in a **sink**.
To **sink** is to go down or under.
The sun **sinks** below the horizon.
Ships sometimes **sink** in stormy seas.

SISTER

A girl who has the same parents as you do is your **sister**.
Jane is John's **sister**. They have the same mother and father.

SIT

To **sit** is to be seated in some place.
Baby Brother is old enough to **sit** in a chair but Bouncing Baby must **sit** on Mother's lap.
Clarence Cat likes to **sit** by the fire.

SIX

Six is the number after five.
Six is one more than five.
5 + 1 = **6**.

SIXTEEN

Sixteen is the number after fifteen.
Sixteen is six more than ten.
10 + 6 = **16**.

SIZE

Size means how big or how little something is.
Aunty Ivy grows flowers of all **sizes**, big and little.
Tilly Tortoise is larger in **size** than Snowy Snail.

SKI

A **ski** is one of a pair of long, thin pieces of metal fastened to the underside of boots for gliding over snow.
To **ski** is to travel over snow on **skis**.
Bobby Boy's ambition is to **ski** down a mountain.

SKY

The **sky** is the space above the earth. At night the **sky** is dark.
During the day the **sky** looks blue.
We see the sun, the moon and the stars in the **sky**.
Arnold Aircraft flies in the **sky**.

SLEEP

We shut our eyes when we go to **sleep**. We rest our minds and our bodies when we go to **sleep**.
When we **sleep** we are not awake.
People, animals and birds **sleep**.

SLEEVE

A **sleeve** is that part of a dress, jacket or coat which covers part or all of the arm.
Belinda Ballerina's dress has short **sleeves**.
Farmer Brown's jacket has long **sleeves**.

SLIPPER

A **slipper** is a soft, comfortable shoe that we wear indoors.
Baby Brother has a pair of warm, woollen **slippers**.

SLOW

Snowy Snail takes a long time to get

to the party because he is a **slow-moving** creature. He cannot go fast.
Sometimes a road sign warns drivers to **slow** down because there is danger ahead.

SMALL

Missy Mouse is **small**. She is not large like Elly Elephant.
Baby Brother is **small**. He is not big or tall.

SMILE

Bobby Boy has a **smile** on his face. He has a happy look on his face because he has found his ball.

SNAIL

Snowy **Snail** is a small animal with a coiled shell in which he can hide when danger threatens.
Snowy **Snail** moves very slowly.
Snails live in water or on land.

SNOW

Snow is soft, white flakes of frozen water which fall from the sky in winter.
The children will build a **snowman** from the **snow** that lies on the ground.

SO

So means for that reason.
Digger Dog was hungry, **so** Bobby Boy fed him.
So also means very.
Mother Goose is **so** busy today!

SOCK

A **sock** is a short stocking that covers your foot and the lower part of your leg.
Aunty Ivy is knitting a pair of **socks**.

SOFT

A **soft** thing does not feel hard or rough. Snowflakes, feathers and wool are **soft**.
Clarence Cat's fur is **soft**.
If you speak **softly**, you speak in a quiet, low voice.

SOME

Some is an unstated number of things.
Some children wear short socks.
Some flowers are yellow.
Some sleeves are long; **some** are short.

SOON

Tracy Train will come **soon**.
She will come in a short time.
Bouncing Baby must go to bed **soon**.
He must go to bed before long.

SORRY

The children are very **sorry** that David is ill.
They feel sad that he is ill.
Snowy Snail said, "I am **sorry** I am late but I cannot go any faster."

SOUND

Any noise is a **sound**. We hear **sounds** with our ears.
Sh! Do not make a **sound**.
Bouncing Baby is asleep.

SOUP

Soup is a liquid food made by boiling meat, or fish, or vegetables in water.
Uncle Harry likes beef and vegetable **soup**.

SOUTH

South is a direction. When you face the rising sun in the east, **south** is to the right. **South** is opposite to north.

SPADE

A **spade** is a tool for digging. A **spade** has a blade and a handle.
Father digs the garden with a **spade**.
Baby Brother likes to dig in the sand on the shore with his little **spade**.

SPELL

To **spell** is to write or say the letters of a word in the right order. S U N spells sun.
A **spell** is a short period of time.
In winter we have **spells** of snow.
A **spell** can also be a magic charm cast by a fairy, or a witch, or a wizard.
Some **spells** are good; some are evil.

SPIDER

Spikey **Spider** is a small animal with eight legs and no wings.
Spiders spin webs to catch insects for food.

SPLASH

Bouncing Baby likes to **splash** in his bath. He makes the water fly about.
Nellie Neighbour's dress is **splashed** with green paint.
You would hear a big **splash** if Elly Elephant jumped in a swimming pool.

SPOON

A **spoon** is a little bowl with a long handle. We eat liquid food like soup with a **spoon**.
Mother feeds Bouncing Baby with a **spoon**.

SPORT

Sport is a game or an activity or a pastime that you either watch or take part in yourself. Swimming, skiing, tennis, golf and soccer are popular **sports**.

SPRING

Spring is the first season of the year.
A **spring** is a small trickle of water coming from the earth.
To **spring** is to leap or jump.
Will Clarence Cat **spring** at Missy Mouse?

SQUARE

A **square** is a shape with four sides that are the same length. The spaces on a chessboard are **squares**.

SQUIRREL

A **squirrel** is a small animal with grey, red or dark brown fur and a long, bushy tail.
Squeaky **Squirrel** lives in a tree and eats nuts. He stores away nuts to eat in winter.

STABLE

A **stable** is a building where horses are kept and fed.
Filly Foal lives in a **stable**.

STAMP

A **stamp** is a small piece of printed, gummed paper to be stuck on parcels or envelopes so the Post Office will send them where we want them to go.
If you **stamp** your feet you bang them on the ground.

STAR

A **star** is a twinkling point of light seen in the sky at night. Some of the **stars** are larger than the sun but they look small because they are so very far away.

STATION

A **station** is a regular stopping place for buses or trains.
Bobby Boy must meet Aunty Ivy at the railway **station**.
A **station** is a building or a place that is used for some particular purpose. Most large towns have fire **stations**, police **stations** and petrol **stations**.

STATUE

A **statue** is a figure of a person or an animal carved in wood or stone, or cast in metal.
The **Statue** of Liberty is a famous monument in New York Harbour.

STEEPLE

A **steeple** is a high tower on the roof of a church. The tall, pointed part of a **steeple** is called a spire.

STEP

To **step** is to move your feet as you do when you walk, run, skip or dance.

Father is tall and takes long **steps**; Baby Brother is small and takes short **steps**.

STOP

To **stop** is to cease, or bring to an end something you are doing.

Big Bus will **stop** at the bus station.

Baby Brother will soon **stop** crying.

You must **stop**, look and listen before you cross the road.

STORY

A **story** is an account of happenings that are true, or happenings that are made up to entertain the listener or reader.

The sailor told the **story** of his life at sea.

Have you read the **story** of Oliver Twist?

STRANGER

A **stranger** is somebody that you know nothing about, so you must never go anywhere with a **stranger**.

STREET

A **street** is a road in a town or city that usually has shops and houses on both sides.

Traffic travels along the **street** so you must be careful when you cross a **street**.

STRING

String is thick thread, or thin cord, rope or wire.

We tie packages with **string**.

Vicky Violin has four **strings** made of thin wire.

Baby Brother uses a **string** to fly his kite.

A number of things in a line or row is called a **string**.

A **string** of racehorses galloped down the track.

STRIPE

A **stripe** is a long, narrow band.

Tiggy Tiger has **stripes**.

Zebby Zebra has black and white **stripes**.

Benjamin Butcher has an apron with blue and white **stripes**.

STRONG

Strong means powerful and not weak.

Bobby Boy is a **strong** boy. He can lift heavy things.

Elly Elephant is **strong**. She can carry very heavy loads.

Garlic and onions have a **strong** smell and a **strong** flavour.

STUDENT

A **student** is someone who studies.

Bobby Boy is a **student** in Tommy Teacher's school.

A person who studies music is a **student** of music.

SUBMARINE

A **submarine** is a vessel that can sail under water.

SUDDEN

Sudden means quick and unexpected.
A **sudden** noise woke Bouncing Baby.

SUGAR

Sugar is what we put in food to make it sweet. **Sugar** is made from the juice of **sugar** cane or **sugar** beet.

SUMMER

Summer is the warmest season of the year and comes between spring and autumn.

SUN

The **sun** is the brightest object in the sky. The **sun** shines during the day and gives us light and heat.
The earth travels round the **sun** once every 365¼ days.

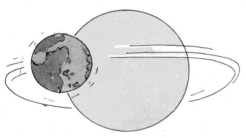

SUNDAY

Sunday is the first day of the week.
Sunday comes after Saturday.

SUPERMARKET

A **supermarket** is a large, self-service shop which sells food and household goods.

SURGEON

A **surgeon** is a doctor who performs operations.
A **surgeon** took out Jill's tonsils.

SURPRISE

A **surprise** is what you get when something unexpected happens. Belinda Ballerina was **surprised** to see Elly Elephant dancing on her toes.

SWALLOW

A **swallow** is a small bird with long wings and a forked tail. A **swallow** can fly swiftly.
When we eat we **swallow** our food and drink.

SWAN

A **swan** is a large water-bird with short legs and a long, curving neck.

SWEATER

A **sweater** is a warm garment worn on the upper part of the body. Aunty Ivy is knitting a **sweater** for Bobby Boy.

SWEEP

To **sweep** means to brush with a broom to make something clean. Natalie Niece likes to **sweep** the floor.
Bobby Boy will **sweep** the path.

SWEET

Things that taste like sugar or honey are **sweet**
Sweet also means charming or pleasant.
Bouncing Baby is a **sweet** child.
Some flowers have a **sweet** smell.

SWIM

To **swim** is to make your body move through water. People **swim** by moving their arms and legs. Daffy Duck and Gracie Gosling **swim** with their feet.
Fish **swim** by moving their fins and tails.

Tt

TABLE

A **table** is a piece of furniture with a smooth, flat top on legs.
A list of facts and figures is also called a **table**. Bobby Boy learned the multiplication **tables**.

TACK

A **tack** is a short, pointed nail with a broad, flat head.
Farmer Brown used **tacks** to fasten the sign to the fence.

TADPOLE

A **tadpole** is a baby frog. It hatches from frogs' spawn and has to live in water. Then it grows legs and can go on land as a frog.

TAG

A **tag** is a small label tied to a thing to tell something about it.
In a game of **tag** one person chases the others until he touches one of them who then does the chasing.

TAIL

The end or back part of anything is called the **tail**.
Missy Mouse has a long **tail**.
A tadpole loses its **tail** when it turns into a frog.

TAILOR

A **tailor** is a person who makes coats and suits.
Dad asked the **tailor** to mend a tear in the sleeve of his jacket.

TAKE

To **take** is to get hold of something or to lead or carry something from one place to another.
Bobby Boy will **take** Digger Dog for a walk.

TALE

A **tale** is a story. Tommy Teacher told the children an exciting **tale** about a haunted castle.

TALK

When we **talk** we say something.
Aunty Ivy likes to **talk** about the flowers in her garden.

TALL

Tall is high.
George Giraffe is a **tall** animal.
A sky-scraper is a **tall** building.
Father is a **tall** man but he is not as **tall** as Geoffrey Giant.

TAME

Some animals are **tame**. They are no longer wild but have become gentle and used to being with people.
Some birds are so **tame** they will take food from your hand.

TANK

A **tank** is a large container used to hold liquid or gas.
Big Bus has a petrol **tank**.
Timmy **Tank** is an armoured, military vehicle with caterpillar tracks so he can travel over rough ground.

TASK

A **task** is a piece of work that has to be done.
Bobby Boy's **task** is to feed Digger Dog each day.

TASTE

We use our tongues to **taste** the flavour of food or drink.
Baby Brother likes the sweet **taste** of ice cream.

TEA

Tea is a hot drink made by pouring boiling water over the dried and shredded leaves of the **tea** plant.
Some people put milk and sugar in **tea** to make it taste sweet.

TEACHER

A **teacher** is a person who shows you how to do something and helps you to learn.
Tommy **Teacher** is teaching the children to make a kite.

TEAM

A **team** is a group of people or animals who do something together.
A **team** of horses can pull a heavy load.

TEAR

1) A **tear** (rhyming with hair) is a jagged rip in something. Father has a **tear** in the sleeve of his jacket.
2) A **tear** (rhyming with deer) is a drop of salty water that falls from our eyes when we cry because we are hurt or sad.

TEASPOON

A **teaspoon** is a small spoon. We usually stir tea with a **teaspoon**.
Baby Brother uses a **teaspoon** to eat his food.

TELEPHONE

A **telephone** is an instrument with which we can talk to people who are far away. When we speak into a **telephone** our voices are carried through wires by electricity to the other person's **telephone**.

TELEVISION

A **television** is an electrical device which brings sounds and pictures through the air to our homes from events happening a long way away.

TEN

The number **ten** is one more than nine. 9 + 1 = **10**.
Two fives make **ten**. 2 x 5 = **10**.

TENT

A **tent** is a canvas shelter held up by poles.
When people go camping they often sleep in **tents**.

TERM

A **term** is a set period of time.
Most schools have three **terms** a year.

TEST

A **test** is an examination or trial. Tommy Teacher gave the children a maths **test**.
Dad **tested** the lawn-mower to see if it would work.

THANK

To **thank** someone is to tell them you are grateful for something.
When you receive help or a gift you should say, "**Thank you**."
Aunty Ivy will **thank** Bobby Boy for the present he has given her.

THAT

That is used to mean the person or thing further away from us.
This boy here is tall but **that** boy over there is small.
That can be used instead of which. Show me the book **that** you like best.

THE

The refers to a particular person or thing.
The toy I bought from this toyshop is broken. **The** boy who helped me lives there.

THEATRE

A **theatre** is a building where plays are acted.
The children went to a **theatre** to watch the pantomime.

THEIR

Their means belonging to them. The children brush **their** hair and clean **their** teeth and shine **their** shoes before they go to school.

THEN

Then means at that time, or next, or soon after.
The party begins at four o' clock. Will you be there **then**?
The lightning flashed and **then** we heard the thunder.

THERE

There means not here but in, or at, or to, some other place.
The park is over **there**. They have swings and roundabouts **there**. Do you want to go **there**?

THEY

They is used to refer to people, or animals or things.
Albert Ape and Mickey Monkey are friends. **They** like each other.

THICK

Thick means not thin. We wear **thick** clothes in cold weather. A **thick** liquid is hard to pour.
Thick also means set close together. Dainty Doll has **thick** hair.

THIEF

A **thief** is someone who steals. **Thieves** take things which belong to other people.

THIN

Thin means not fat or thick. Belinda Ballerina is **thin** but Piggles Pig is fat.
We wear **thin** clothes in hot weather. Spikey Spider hung from a **thin** thread.

THING

A **thing** is any object, or any thought, action or event.
Bobby Boy put all Baby Brother's **things** away for him.
It was a kind **thing** to do.

THINK

To **think** is to believe or to have ideas or opinions in our minds.
If we want to learn or do anything we must **think**. I hear thunder! Do you **think** it will rain?

THIRD

Third is after second in a list.
March is the **third** month in the year.
If you divide something equally between three people each person has a **third** of it.

THIRSTY

If you are **thirsty** you want a drink. Bouncing Baby drinks milk when he is **thirsty**.

THIRTEEN

The number **thirteen** is one more than twelve. 12 + 1 = **13**.
Thirteen is three more than ten. 10 + 3 = **13**.

THIS

THIS WAY

This refers to the person or thing near to you or just spoken about.
This is my friend. We shall go for a walk **this** morning. Shall we go **this** way or that?

THORN

Thorns are sharp points that grow on the stems of some plants. Rose bushes have **thorns**.
Dad tore his sleeve on a **thorn**.

THREAD

Thread is a fine cord made of twisted strands of silk, wool, nylon or cotton. You sew with **thread**.
Spikey Spider hung by a **thread**.
To **thread** is to pass a **thread** through something.
Natalie Niece **threaded** beads to make a necklace.

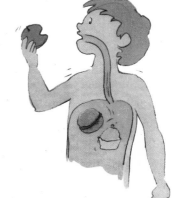

THREE

The number **three** is one more than two. 2 + 1 = **3**.

THROAT

Your **throat** is the first part of your neck and food and drink go down your **throat** when you swallow.
Your **throat** feels dry when you are thirsty.

THROUGH

Through means from one side, or one end, to the other. We look **through** windows and walk **through** doorways.
Tracy Train went **through** the tunnel.
Have you read **through** this book?

THROW

To **throw** is to make something move through the air.
Throw the ball to me and I will catch it and **throw** it back to you.

THUMB

The **thumb** is the shortest and thickest of the five end parts of your hand.

Bouncing Baby sucks his **thumb** when he is tired.

THUNDER

Thunder is the loud noise which usually follows a flash of lightning during a storm.

THURSDAY

Thursday is the fifth day of the week.

Thursday comes after Wednesday.

TICKET

A **ticket** is a piece of paper or card which shows the price of something. You buy a **ticket** to see a show or to travel somewhere.

TIDY

Mother Goose keeps her home **tidy**. Everything is in its proper place and there is no mess.

The children will **tidy** the room after the party.

TIE

If you **tie** a thing, you fasten it. Can you **tie** your shoelaces?

A **necktie** is a narrow piece of cloth worn round the neck and **tied** in a knot or a bow.

If a contest ends in a **tie** the scores are equal.

TIGER

A **tiger** is a fierce wild animal. Tiggy **Tiger** has sharp teeth and black stripes on his yellow fur.

TIME

Time measures how long something lasts. A minute is a short **time**; a year is a long **time**.

We measure **time** with clocks and watches.

A **time** is an occasion.

A party is a **time** for having fun.

TINY

Tiny means very small.

An ant is a **tiny** insect.

TIRED

If you are **tired** you feel weary and need a rest.

Bouncing Baby goes to sleep when he is **tired**.

TISSUE

Tissue is the living matter of which plants and animals are made.

A paper **tissue** is a soft, disposable handkerchief.

TITLE

The **title** of a book, story, poem, painting or song is its name. What is the **title** of your favourite book? The **title** of a person is the word used to show their rank, occupation or position in life - Captain, Queen, Doctor, Mr, Mrs, Master and Miss are all **titles**.

TO

To means in the direction of, or as far as, or for the purpose of.
Children go **to** school **to** learn.
Tommy Teacher is talking **to** Bobby Boy.
Natalie Niece knows how **to** count **to** a hundred.

TOAST

Toast is bread which is scorched to make it crisp and brown.
Some people eat **toast** for breakfast.
Sometimes we **toast** marshmallows.

TODAY

Today is this very day. It was fine yesterday but it is raining **today**.

TOE

A **toe** is one of the five end parts of your foot.
Belinda Ballerina dances on her **toes**.

TOGETHER

Together means with each other.
Daniel Dwarf and Eric Elf play **together**.
Farmer Brown put all his cows **together** in one field.

TOMATO

A **tomato** is a juicy red or yellow fruit with many seeds.
Tomatoes are good to eat with lettuce and cucumber.

TOMORROW

Tomorrow is the day after today.
If today is Wednesday, **tomorrow** will be Thursday.

TONGUE

A **tongue** is the soft, moveable, piece of flesh in the mouth used for tasting and eating and, by people, for speaking.
Frankie Frog catches flies with his long **tongue**.

TOO

Too means also or as well.
Bouncing Baby is tired and hungry **too**.
Too also means more than enough.
Elly Elephant ate **too** much.

TOOL

A **tool** is anything that is used in doing work.
A spade is a **tool** for digging.
A pen is a **tool** for writing.
A saw is a **tool** for cutting wood.

TOOTH

A **tooth** is one of the hard, white, pointed parts that grow in the mouths of people and most animals. They are used for biting and chewing and you should clean your **teeth** every day.
Christopher Crocodile has very sharp **teeth**.

TOP

The **top** of something is its highest point or part.
Albert Ape and Champ Chimp climbed to the **top** of the tree.
A **top** is a toy that spins round.

TORN

If something is **torn** it has a tear or rip in it.
Dad's sleeve is **torn**. He **tore** it on a sharp thorn.

TORTOISE

Tilly **Tortoise** is a slow-moving animal who lives on land.
Tilly **Tortoise** has a hard, thick shell on her back.

TOUCH

To **touch** is to feel something with any part of your body but usually your fingers or hand.
Do not **touch** Nellie Neighbour's door because the paint is still wet.

TOW

To **tow** is to pull or drag something along with a chain or rope.
Baby Brother likes to **tow** his toy train along the path.

TOY

A **toy** is something with which to play.
Most children like to play with **toys**.

TRACK

A **track** is a mark left by the movement of a person, animal or thing.
Bobby Boy's skis left a **track** in the snow.
Trains run on railway **tracks**.
A rough road or path is also called a **track** and so is a roadway or path used especially for racing.

TRAFFIC

Traffic means the coming and going of people and vehicles along a land, sea or air route.
It is dangerous to cross a street when there is a lot of **traffic**.

TRAIN

A **train** is a line of railway coaches or carriages pulled by an engine.

TRAINERS

Trainers are shoes with flat, rubber soles. Bobby Boy can run very fast when he is wearing **trainers**.

TRANSPORT

To **transport** people or things means to take them from one place to another. Passengers and goods can be **transported** by road, rail, sea and air.

TRAVEL

To **travel** is to make a journey or to go from place to place.
Arnold Aircraft hopes to **travel** round the world.

TRAY

A **tray** is a flat piece of metal, wood or plastic with a shallow rim round it that is used for carrying things.
Chief Chef carried a bowl of hot soup on a **tray**.

TREASURE

reasure is a store or collection of
aluables. Pirates buried **treasure**
n a desert island.
o treasure something is to value it
ery highly. Baby Brother
reasures his toy train.

REE

rigger Tree is a large, leafy plant
ith a woody trunk and branches.
queaky Squirrel collects the acorns
om oak **trees**.

RIAL

trial is an examination in a court
f law to decide the innocence or
uilt of a prisoner.
trial is also a testing or trying out
f something. Bobby Boy gave his
te a **trial** to see if it would fly.

TRIANGLE

A **triangle** is a shape with three
straight sides and three corners. It
is also a musical instrument made of
a steel rod bent into a **triangle**
and hit with a small steel rod.

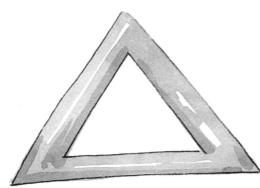

TRIP

A **trip** is a journey or an outing.
The children had a **trip** to the sea.
To **trip** is to catch your foot on
something and stumble or fall.
Daniel Dwarf **tripped** on the mat.

TROUBLE

Trouble is anything that causes
worry, annoyance, concern, pain,
unhappiness, distress, difficulty or
extra work.

TROUSERS

Trousers are clothing worn over
the legs, reaching from the waist to
the knees or ankles.
Baby Brother wears short **trousers**.
Dad wears long **trousers**.

TRUCK

A **truck** is a large vehicle that
carries things from place to place.
Farmer Brown uses a **truck** to
transport his corn to the mill.

TRUNK

A **trunk** is a
large box used
for holding or
carrying
belongings.
An elephant's
nose is also called
a **trunk**. Elly
Elephant picks up
food and water
with her **trunk**.
The main stem or
body of anything
is called a
trunk. Trigger
Tree has a thick **trunk**.

TRUTH

The **truth** is what is true, real or a
fact.
We should always tell the **truth**
because it is wrong to lie and liars
usually get into trouble.

TRY

To **try** is to make an attempt to do
something.
Bobby Boy will **try** to find his ball.
Try also means to test or give a
trial to something.
Try these trainers to see if they fit.

TUESDAY

Tuesday is the third day of the
week.
Tuesday comes after Monday.

TURN

To **turn** is to move round like a spinning top or to change direction. **Turn** left at the next corner.

It can also mean to change or to become. She was shocked and **turned** pale.

When it is your **turn** in the game you can play.

TURTLE

A **turtle** is an animal with a hard shell on its back. It looks like a tortoise but lives in the sea and grows much bigger.

TUSK

A **tusk** is a large, pointed tooth which some animals have. Elephants, warthogs and wild boars have a pair of **tusks** and so do walruses.

TUTOR

A **tutor** is a private teacher who teaches students individually or in small groups.

David had a **tutor** when he was ill and could not go to school.

TWELVE

The number **twelve** is one more than eleven. 11 + 1 = **12**.

There are **twelve** months in a year.

TWENTY

The number **twenty** is one more than nineteen. 19 + 1 = **20**.

Two tens make **twenty**.

2 x 10 = **20**.

TWIN

A **twin** is one of the two children or animals born to the same mother at one time.

Twins sometimes look alike.

TWINKLE

To **twinkle** is to shine and sparkle with quick flashes of light. Stars **twinkle** in the night sky.

Dad's eyes **twinkle** when he laughs.

TWIST

To **twist** is to wind or turn or to bend a thing out of shape.

Aunty Ivy **twists** her ring on her finger.

This path **twists** through the trees.

TWO

The number **two** is one more than one.

1 + 1 = **2**.

We have **two** hands and **two** thumbs.

Birds have **two** wings.

TYPEWRITER

A **typewriter** is a machine which prints letters and figures on paper when the keys on the keyboard are pressed individually.

A person who uses a **typewriter** is called a typist.

TYRE

A **tyre** is an air-inflated, rubber tube which fits round the rim of a wheel.

Nice Nurse cannot ride her bicycle because the front **tyre** has a puncture.

Uu

UGLY

If something is **ugly** it is not pretty to look at.

In some fairy stories witches and trolls have **ugly** faces. Do you know the story of the **ugly** duckling who became a beautiful swan?

UMBRELLA

An **umbrella** is a cloth-covered, metal frame on a stick you hold over your head to shelter you from the rain.

Umberto **Umbrella** is shaped like a mushroom but can fold up.

UNCLE

My father's brother is my **uncle**.
My mother's brother is my **uncle**.
My aunt's husband is my **uncle** too.

UNDER

Under is below or less than.
Clarence Cat hides **under** the bed.
Submarines can sail **under** the water.
The storm lasted **under** five minutes.

UNHAPPY

If you are **unhappy** you feel sad.
Bobby Boy was **unhappy** when he lost his ball.
David was **unhappy** when he was ill.

UNTIE

To **untie** means to undo or unfasten.
Some knots are easy to **untie**.
Remember to **untie** your shoe-laces before you take off your shoes.

UNTIL

Until means up to the time of or to the time when.
Farmer Brown works from morning **until** night.
Bobby Boy played football **until** dinner was ready.

UP

Up means on high, or to go to a higher place, or to be at or near the top. Squeaky Squirrel is **up** his tree.
Arnold Aircraft flew **up** into the sky.

UPON

Upon means on the top of something.
Put the plates **upon** the shelf and the cups **upon** the table.

UPSTAIRS

Upstairs means not on the ground floor, or beyond a staircase.
Bobby Boy sleeps **upstairs**.
Dad walked **upstairs** from the cellar.

USE

To **use** is to make something do a job of work for some purpose.
We **use** a knife to cut things.
We **use** our minds to think.

USUAL

Usual means what often happens or something done so often it is well-known.
Nice Nurse had her **usual** happy smile on her face.
It is **usual** for Bouncing Baby to drink milk.
Daniel Dwarf met Eric Elf at their **usual** meeting place.

Vv

VACANT

Vacant means empty and unoccupied.
That house is **vacant**. Nobody lives there and there is nothing inside.

VACATION

A **vacation** is a holiday.
Bobby Boy had a week's **vacation** from school, so Uncle Harry took a week's **vacation** from work. They spent their **vacation** at the seaside.

VALENTINE

A **valentine** is a card or a gift for someone you love which is sent to them on **St Valentine's Day**, February 14th.

VALLEY

A **valley** is the low land that lies between two hills or mountains.
Some **valleys** have rivers or streams running through them.

VALUE

Value means the price, importance, or usefulness of something.
What is the **value** of Aunty Ivy's gold ring?
Healthy people recognise the **value** of regular exercise.

VARNISH

Varnish is a sticky liquid that is painted on a surface to protect it.
It dries to a hard, shiny surface.
Natalie Niece puts pink **varnish** on her finger nails.
The floors at Tommy Teacher's school are covered with **varnish**.

VASE

A **vase** can be used as an ornament or for holding flowers.
Aunty Ivy put some red roses in a pretty, blue **vase**.

VEGETABLE

A **vegetable** is a plant that we grow for food and which is not a fruit.
Peas, beans, lettuces, potatoes, carrots, cabbages and onions are **vegetables**.

VEHICLE

A **vehicle** is a car, wagon, lorry, bus, cart, or sleigh, or any other means used for carrying goods or people from place to place on land
Andy Ambulance, Jonty Jeep and Timmy Tank are **vehicles**.

VEIL

A **veil** is a piece of very thin material worn over the head or face as part of a head-dress.
Dainty Doll has a **veil** on her favourite hat.
A **veil** can also be worn to hide or protect the face.

VERSE

Verse is another name for poetry.
A **verse** is a group of lines from a song or poem, or a short section from a chapter in the Bible.
Do you know the first **verse** of 'Mary Had a Little Lamb'?

VERY

Very means extremely.
It is **very** cold today.
Mother Goose is always **very** busy

IEW

view means to look at.
armer Brown likes to view his
elds from the top of the hill.
e scene, or all that he sees before
m, is called a view.

ILLAGE

village is a group of houses,
metimes with a church or shops,
at is much smaller than a town.

INEGAR

inegar is a sour liquid made from
ples or grapes and is used for
vouring and pickling food.

IOLIN

cky Violin is a small musical
strument with four strings played
ith a bow or sometimes by
ucking.
violin is held
der the chin
hen it is
eing
ayed.

ISIT

visit is to go or come to see
meone or something.
rcy Peacock will visit his friend
ter Penguin.
affy Duck and Lucy Lamb visited
e circus last week.
visit is also a short stay.

VITAMIN

A vitamin is any of a number of
special substances found in food that
are needed to make our bodies
strong and healthy. Vitamins are
named after letters of the alphabet.
Oranges contain vitamin C.
Vitamins are found especially in
raw fruits and vegetables, fish, milk,
butter and cereals.

VOICE

Your voice is the sound from your
mouth when you speak or sing.
The referee's voice was loud.
Natalie Niece likes singing because
she has a sweet singing voice.

VOLCANO

A volcano is a mountain with an
opening at the top, called a crater,
through which steam, gases and hot
melted rock are thrown out.

VOLUME

Volume is the amount of space
something occupies or the amount of
room inside it. The volume of a
house is more than the volume of a
dog kennel. What is the volume of
your toy-box?
A volume is also a book, or one of
a set of books.
Bobby Boy owns several volumes.

VOTE

A vote is your stated choice or wish
in a matter that concerns you.
People vote by raising a hand, by
speaking, or by writing on a piece of
paper called a ballot paper.
The team voted for Bobby Boy to
be captain.

VOYAGE

A voyage is a journey by sea or
air.
To voyage is to travel or make a
journey, especially to a far-away
place.
Sidney Ship's voyage across the
ocean will take five days.

VOWEL

The letters a, e, i, o, u, and sometimes y, are vowels. There are five
vowels in the word mysterious.

Ww

WADDLE

To **waddle** is to walk with short steps and rock from side to side. Daffy Duck and Goosey Gander both **waddle**.

WADE

To **wade** is to walk through water. Do you like to **wade** in the sea?

WAFER

A **wafer** is a very thin, crisp biscuit. We usually eat **wafers** with ice-cream.

WAG

Digger Dog **wags** his tail when he is happy. He moves his tail from side to side.

WAGON (also spelt WAGGON)

A **wagon** is a sturdy, four-wheeled cart or truck for transporting heavy loads by rail or road.
Road **wagons** are sometimes pulled by horses.

WAIST

Your **waist** is the middle part of your body, between your ribs and hips.
Farmer Brown wears a leather belt around his **waist**.

WAIT

To **wait** is to stay where you are until someone comes or something happens. The time spent **waiting** is called a **wait**.
Daniel Dwarf will **wait** until his friend, Eric Elf, arrives. If he is late Daniel will have a long **wait**.

WAITER

A **waiter** is a man who serves food or drink to guests in a hotel or restaurant.

WAITRESS

A **waitress** is a woman who serves food or drink to guests in a hotel or restaurant.

WAKE

To **wake** is to stop sleeping.
Father **wakes** at six every morning. If he makes too much noise he will **wake** Bouncing Baby.

WALK

To **walk** is to move about on foot at a slower pace than when running.
Bobby Boy usually **walks** to school.

WALL

A **wall** is any one side of a building or room, or any solidly-built fence. **Walls** are usually built of brick or stone.
There is a mirror on the bathroom **wall**.
Humpty Dumpty sat on a **wall**.

WALLET

A **wallet** folds open and shut and is used for carrying paper money, credit cards and personal papers. Uncle Harry has a photograph of Bobby Boy in his **wallet**.

WANT

Want means to wish for. Natalie Niece **wants** a new umbrella.
Want also means to be in need of. During a famine, people are in **want** of food.

WARDROBE

A **wardrobe** is a room or cupboard where clothes are kept and is also the stock of clothes a person has.
Aunty Ivy is shopping for her winter **wardrobe**.

WARM

Warm means neither hot nor cold. Clarence Cat drinks **warm** milk.
To **warm** means to heat a little. Dad will **warm** himself by the fire.

WAS

We use the word **was** when we talk about something in the past.
Dad **was** asleep but now he is awake. Yesterday it **was** fine but today it is raining.

WASH

We **wash** things to make them clean using water or special liquids.
Did you **wash** your hands and face this morning?
Farmer Brown **washes** Trevor Tractor every week.

WASTE

Waste is rubbish or things that cannot be used again.
Tommy Teacher threw his **waste** paper into the bin.
To **waste** is to make poor or careless use of something.
You should not **waste** food by taking more than you can eat.

WATCH

A **watch** is a small clock that can be worn on the wrist, carried in a pocket or worn on one's clothing.
To **watch** means to look at something.
Bobby Boy likes to **watch** his kite fly high in the sky.

WATER

Living things cannot survive without **water**. It is the liquid that fills the oceans, seas, rivers, lakes and ponds. Rain is **water**.
To **water** is to put **water** on plants or to give animals **water** to drink.

WATERFALL

A **waterfall** is a stream of water falling from a high place.

WAVE

A **wave** is a line of moving water rising and falling on the surface of the sea.
Sidney Ship was tossed by **waves**. If you **wave** to someone you move your hand to and fro. Brian Baker **waved** to Aunty Ivy as she passed.

WAX

Wax is the soft, yellowish substance bees make to use for honeycombs.
Beeswax and other similar substances are used to make candles and polish.

WAY

A **way** is a path, road, track or direction. Look both **ways** before you cross the road.
A **way** can also be a method or a distance.
Singing is one **way** of making music.
The moon is a long **way** away.

WE

We means either just you and me or us together with some others.
We must clean our teeth before **we** go to bed.
We all play with the toys in our house.

WEAK

If something is **weak** it is not strong.
The fever made David **weak**.
Mother likes **weak** tea.
A **weak** rope can easily be broken.

WEALTH

Wealth is a large amount of money or valuable possessions.
A person of **wealth** is very rich.

WEAR

To **wear** a thing is to have it on your body. We **wear** warm clothing in cold weather. Nellie Neighbour **wears** a gold ring on her finger. **Wear** also means to rub away or damage through use. Dad walked to work and **wore** a hole in his shoe.

WEATHER

Weather is how hot, cold, wet or still the air is outside at any one time or place.
The air is warm in hot **weather**.

WEDDING

A **wedding** is a ceremony at which a man and a woman are married and so become husband and wife.

WEDNESDAY

Wednesday is the fourth day of the week.
Wednesday comes after Tuesday.

WEED

A **weed** is a wild plant that grows where it is not wanted. **Weeds** often prevent other plants from growing.
Aunty Ivy pulls the **weeds** out of her garden.

WEEK

A **week** is a period of seven days, one after another. Uncle Harry went on holiday for a **week**.

WEEKDAY

A **weekday** is any day of the week except Saturday and Sunday. Monday, Tuesday, Wednesday, Thursday and Friday are the **weekdays**.

WEEKEND

The **weekend** is Saturday and Sunday and is a holiday for many people.

WEEP

To **weep** is to cry tears.
When Baby Brother grazed his knee he started to **weep**.

WEIGH

When you **weigh** something you find out how heavy it is.
Mother will **weigh** Bouncing Baby at the weekend.

WELCOME

To **welcome** means to greet or receive gladly. Eddy Eagle will **welcome** Snowy Snail when he arrives.
Sunshine is **welcome** after a spell of rain.

WELL

To be **well** is to be in good health.
David is now **well**. He no longer has a fever.
Well also means in a correct or satisfactory manner or way.
Bobby Boy works **well**.
Belinda Ballerina dances very **well**.
A **well** is also a deep hole dug in the ground to get water, oil or gas.

WELLINGTONS

Wellingtons are knee-high, rubber boots for keeping our feet dry in wet weather.

WERE

We use the word **were** when we talk about more than one thing in the past.
The children **were** playing in the garden and **were** late for school.
Those trees **were** once small but now they are tall.

WEST

West is the direction opposite to east. The sun sets in the **west**.

WET

Wet means soaked or covered with water or other liquid.
Digger Dog got **wet** in the rain.
Wet also means not yet dry.
The ink is still **wet**.

WHALE

A **whale** is a huge, sea animal that is shaped like a fish. Some **whales** are larger than any other animal in the world.

WHAT

What is a word we use when asking questions. **What** time is it?
What would you like to do today?
What also means that which and anything that.
If you know **what** you want you may take it and I will keep **what** is left.

WHEAT

Wheat is a plant that produces the grain from which flour and bread, as well as many breakfast cereals, are made. Farmer Brown grows **wheat**.

WHEEL

A **wheel** is a round frame that turns on its axle or centre.
Wheels help things move more easily.
Big Bus, Trevor Tractor and Tracy Train all run on **wheels**.

WHEELBARROW

A **wheelbarrow** is a small cart with a single wheel at the front, two legs at the back and two handles to lift so that it can easily be pushed along.
Wheely **Wheelbarrow** carries small loads.

WHEN

When means at what time or at the time that.
When does the party begin? It will start **when** the guests arrive.

WHERE

Where means in or at what place.
Where does Digger Dog sleep?
Where shall we meet?
Where also means to or from what place.
Where are you going now?
Where did you get that book?

WHICH

Which means what one or that.
Which girl won the race?
Choose the book **which** you like best.

WHILE

A **while** means a period of time. Eric Elf kept Daniel Dwarf waiting a short **while**.
While also means during the time that. **While** he was waiting it began to rain.

WHISKER

A **whisker** is any of the long, stiff hairs growing near the mouths of cats and other animals.
Clarence Cat has long **whiskers**.
The hairs that grow on a man's face are also called **whiskers**.
Chief Chef shaves off his **whiskers** every morning.

WHISPER

To **whisper** is to speak in a soft, low voice. While Bouncing Baby is asleep the whole family **whispers** as they do not want to wake him.

WHISTLE

To **whistle** is to make a clear, shrill sound by forcing your breath through almost closed lips, or by blowing through a hollow instrument which produces whistling sounds.
Bobby Boy **whistled** for Digger Dog.
Tommy Teacher blew a **whistle** when playtime was over.

WHITE

White is the colour of fresh snow.
Nice Nurse wears a **white** apron.
Brock Badger has a **white** face with two black stripes.

WHO

We use the word **who** when asking about people.
Who is your best friend?
Who is coming to the party?
Who also means that.
The boy **who** whistled is my cousin.

WHOLE

Whole means complete with nothing missing or broken.
Aunty Ivy bought a **whole** set of dishes at the market.
The **whole** family watched Piggles Pig eat a **whole** pie.

WHOM

Whom means what person or which people. **Whom** do you like best?
To **whom** shall I send these invitations?

WHY

Why means for what reason.
Why is Bouncing Baby crying?
Why can be used to show surprise.
Why! Snowy Snail is here on time!

WIDE

If something is **wide** it is broad not narrow. Bobby Boy has to cross a **wide** street to go to school.
Wide also means as far open as possible. When you visit the dentist you open your mouth **wide**.

WIFE

A **wife** is a married woman. A woman becomes a **wife** when she marries.

WILD

Many animals are **wild**, not tame like cows and sheep which are used to being with people. Tigers and lions are **wild** animals.
Some plants are **wild**. They are not planted by people but grow wherever they can in fields and woods.

WILL

We use the word **will** to ask or tell about something in the future.
Will it rain today? No. It **will** be a fine, sunny day.
Will you come to the circus? I **will** be there at six o' clock. I am sure you **will** see acrobats and clowns.

WILLOW

A **willow** is a tree or shrub, often found near water, with long, narrow, drooping leaves and long branches which bend easily. The wood from **willows** is used for baskets, furniture and cricket and baseball bats.

WIN

To **win** is to come first in a game or contest. I think Bobby Boy's team will **win** the football match.
The fastest runner usually **wins** the race.
David **won** a painting competition.

WIND (rhyming with pinned)
Wind is air that is moving.
The **wind** blew the leaves from the trees.

WIND (rhyming with mind)
To **wind** means to twist and turn.
The river **winds** its way to the sea.

WINDMILL

A **windmill** is a mill with fanlike sails on top which are pushed round by the wind to grind corn or to pump water or to generate electricity.

WINDOW

A **window** is an opening in a wall or roof of a building to let in light or air or to provide a view.
Windows are usually filled with glass or clear plastic.
Ships, trains, cars and many other vehicles have **windows**.

WINTER

Winter is the fourth season of the year coming after autumn and before spring.

WIRE

Wire is a bendable strand or thread of metal which has many uses.
Cages and fences are often made of **wire**.
When you telephone someone your voice travels through a telephone **wire**. **Wires** carry electricity to where it is needed.

WISE

A **wise** person has a lot of knowledge and uses it to make sensible decisions and give helpful advice.

WISH

To **wish** is to very much want or hope for a thing.
Elly Elephant has a **wish**. She **wishes** she could dance on her toes.
The children **wished** Tommy Teacher a Happy Birthday.

WITCH

We read of **witches** in fairy tales. A **witch** is a woman who is supposed to have magic powers which she often uses to cast evil spells.
Tommy Teacher drew a picture of a **witch** on her broomstick.

WITH

This word is used to show nearness or the use of something.
Jack is **with** Jill. They are walking together.
Chief Chef cut the bread **with** a knife. You see **with** your eyes and taste **with** your tongue.

WITNESS

If you see something happen you **witness** it. The policeman **witnessed** the accident.
A **witness** gives evidence at a trial in a court of law and takes an oath to tell the truth about what he or she has seen.

WOLF

A **wolf** is a wild animal, very much like a large dog, that lives and hunts in packs. **Wolves** can be very fierce and greedy.

WOMAN

A **woman** is a grown-up, female person. Aunty Ivy is a **woman**. Natalie Niece will be a **woman** when she grows up.

WOOD

Wood is the solid part of a tree under the bark and is used for making houses, furniture, boats and many other things.
Vicky Violin is made of **wood**.

WORD

A **word** is a group of letters so arranged that they have a meaning. **Words** can be written or spoken. Have you read all the **words** in this dictionary?
Speak up! I didn't hear a **word**.

WORK

Work is the effort needed to make or do anything. **Work** is also employment in a job. Nice Nurse **works** in a hospital.

WORLD

The **world** is the earth and everything there is on it.
The **world** is round.
Some ships sail round the **world**.

WORM

A **worm** is a long, thin, legless animal that lives in the ground. Birds like to eat **worms**.

WORRY

To **worry** is to feel anxious or troubled. If you are late coming home your parents will **worry**.

WORSE

Worse means something not as good as something else or that something is not being done as well as before.
Eric Elf was quite ill yesterday but he is **worse** today.
The tap is dripping **worse** than ever.

WORTH

A thing of **worth** has value, importance or usefulness.
What is Aunty Ivy's necklace **worth**?
Good health is **worth** more than great wealth.
A saw has to be sharp to be of any **worth**.

WOULD

Would means wished to or was willing or determined to do something.
Bobby Boy said he **would** feed Digger Dog.
Snowy Snail **would** go to the party even though he was feeling ill.

WOUND

A **wound** is any hurt or injury caused to a person or an animal by a cut, a burn, a blow or a shot. Luckily, the graze on Baby Brother's knee is only a small **wound**.

WRAP

If you **wrap** something you fold some kind of material around it. Mother **wrapped** Bouncing Baby in a warm blanket.
Bobby Boy **wrapped** Dad's present.

WRECK

A **wreck** is what is left of anything that has been destroyed or damaged badly.
The waves tossed the **wreck** of a ship on to the rocks.
To **wreck** is to ruin or destroy a thing.

WREN

A **wren** is a small songbird which often builds its nest near houses.
Wrens are brown and have short tails.

WRING

To **wring** is to twist and squeeze hard.
Wring out your wet clothes and hang them up to dry.

WRIST

The **wrist** is the joint where the hand joins the arm.
Uncle Harry wears a watch on his left **wrist**.
Natalie Niece wears a bracelet on her right **wrist**.

WRITE

When we **write** we put letters, words, or figures on paper, or some other surface, so that they can be read.
Bobby Boy has **written** a letter and now he will **write** a story.

WRONG

Wrong means not right or good. It is **wrong** to steal or to cheat or to tell lies.
Wrong also means not true or correct.
Bobby Boy gave a **wrong** answer.
That is the **wrong** way to fly a kite.

Xx Yy Zz

XMAS

Xmas is a short word for Christmas.
A sign in a shop said 'Merry **Xmas**'.

X-RAY

An **x-ray** is an invisible ray that can pass through solid things.
Special cameras use **x-rays** to take shadow photographs of our insides.
Doc Doctor studied the **x-ray** of Dad's broken leg.

XYLOPHONE

A **xylophone** is a musical instrument made of wood or metal bars, each of which gives a different note when struck with a small, wooden hammer.

YACHT

A **yacht** is a light, speedy boat with sails which is used for pleasure trips or racing.

YARD

A **yard** is an area of enclosed ground round or near a building which may be used for some special purpose.
Children play in the **school-yard**.
Sidney Ship was built in a **shipyard**.

YAWN

To **yawn** is to open your mouth wide and breathe out with a long, deep sigh when you are sleepy or bored.
Bouncing Baby **yawned** and fell asleep on Mother's lap.

YEAR

A **year** is the time it takes the earth to travel once round the sun.
There are 52 weeks, 12 months or 365¼ days in a **year** but 366 days in a Leap **Year** which comes every fourth **year**.

YEAST

Yeast is used in making bread.
When mixed in a sugary liquid, **yeast** becomes frothy and the air in the tiny bubbles makes the bread rise.

YELL

To **yell** is to scream, shout or cry out loudly because of pain, fear or excitement.
Daniel Dwarf **yelled** when he bruised his knee.
The team **yelled** when Bobby Boy scored the winning goal.

YELLOW

Yellow is a colour.
Carol Canary has **yellow** feathers.
Butter is **yellow**.
Bananas are **yellow**.

YES

Yes means the opposite of no.
Mother said, "**Yes**, you may go to the park."
We say '**Yes**' when we agree.
"**Yes**, there are seven days in a week," says Tommy Teacher.

YESTERDAY

Yesterday means the day before today.
If today is Saturday, **yesterday** was Friday.

YOGHURT

Yoghurt is a thick, creamy food made from milk. Fruit is sometimes added to **yoghurt** as a flavouring.

YOLK

The yellow part of an egg is called the **yolk**.

YOU

You means the person or persons being spoken to or written to.
Dad said, "If **you** yawn once more, **you** will go to bed."
The invitation said, "Will **you** come to my party?"

YOUNG

Young means not old or grown up.
Natalie Niece is a **young** girl.
Filly Foal is a **young** horse.
A sapling is a **young** tree.

YOURSELF

Yourself means just you and no-one else. You can see **yourself** if you look in the mirror.
Did you hurt **yourself** when you fell?

YOUTH

Youth is the time when a person is young. Tommy Teacher told the children tales of his **youth**.
The word **youth** can mean one young man like Bobby Boy or it can mean a group of young people. Natalie Niece is a member of a **youth** orchestra.

ZEBRA

A **zebra** is an African animal like a small horse. Zebby **Zebra** has black and white stripes all over his body.

ZERO

Zero is a number meaning nought, nothing or none at all and is written like this - **0**.
6 - 6 = **0**.
Zero is the point marked as **0** on a thermometer. If the temperature is **zero** it is very cold.

ZIP

A **zip** is a fastener made of two rows of metal or nylon teeth which is shut and opened by a sliding catch. Clothing, luggage and footwear are often fastened by means of **zips**.

ZODIAC

The **zodiac** is an imaginary belt in the heavens, along which the sun, moon and chief planets seem to move.
It is divided into twelve equal parts, named after groups of stars, called the Signs of the **Zodiac**.

ZONE

A **zone** is an area or region used for a particular purpose. A parking **zone** is where parking is permitted.
A **zone** is also any of the five great divisions of the earth's surface.
The Frigid **Zones** within the Arctic and Antarctic Circles are very cold.

ZOO

A **zoo** is where wild animals are kept for people to see and study them.
Albert Ape and George Giraffe are in the **zoo** too.